Modern
SUGAR FLOWERS

Jacqueline Butler

www.sewandso.co.uk

Contents

INTRODUCTION

I started baking as a teenager, creating fancy treats for my family during the holidays. Cookies, cakes and pies, I experimented with them all, to mostly enthusiastic sibling reviews. Working in the kitchen with careful precision made sense to me, and I loved the time watching and learning from my mom.

Those early days led to baking cakes for friends' and family celebrations, and I soon ventured into sprinkles, piping bags and modeling cute animal figurines. I happened upon a book on pulled sugar flowers, and worked my way through all of the blossoms quickly. The process of shaping a simple ball of paste into a stunning, delicate flower was truly magical to me, and I couldn't get enough of the art form! I researched artists whose work I admired, and traveled extensively to learn a solid foundation in making sugar flowers. At home, I practiced these new skills over and over again until I felt confident enough to try new flowers on my own. Over time, I began incorporating sugar flowers into all of my cake designs and developed a personal style that became Petalsweet.

The sugar flowers I create are stylized, and simply my own interpretation of the real thing. The flowers take a bit of practice, but are not overwhelming, because I try to keep extra details as simple as possible. If a flower detail isn't pretty or functional to me, I might change it or even omit it, and that keeps the flower-making process relaxed and fun. I also use simple cutter shapes and veiners across a variety of flowers where possible, and find this helps me work quickly and efficiently. I encourage you to not focus on perfection, but rather on learning how to make flowers that are well crafted. Practice the techniques, and soon you will be creating beautiful flowers with ease.

Petalsweet cakes are clean and modern, with flower arrangements that are full and fresh. I'm so excited to share some favorite flower combinations in the cake project designs, as well as a variety of arranging techniques that work for me across a range of cake sizes and styles. Most of the projects are on small cakes, so if you are new to flower making, you can jump right in and make a beautiful creation for the next birthday or anniversary! If you are more experienced, you can easily scale up to a stunning wedding cake by working several of the arranging techniques into a larger design.

I'm honored to have the wonderful opportunity to travel the world and teach sugar flowers to truly lovely and passionate students. The best parts of class are meeting the students on the first day, who are usually nervous about making sugar flowers, and then the moment later in class when they are smiling and excited because they have created something they love, and they can't wait to make it again.

I hope you find the tips and techniques helpful so you can begin adding beautiful new sugar flowers to your repertoire right away! And I hope all of the projects and photos will inspire you to create your own elegant and charming floral cake designs.

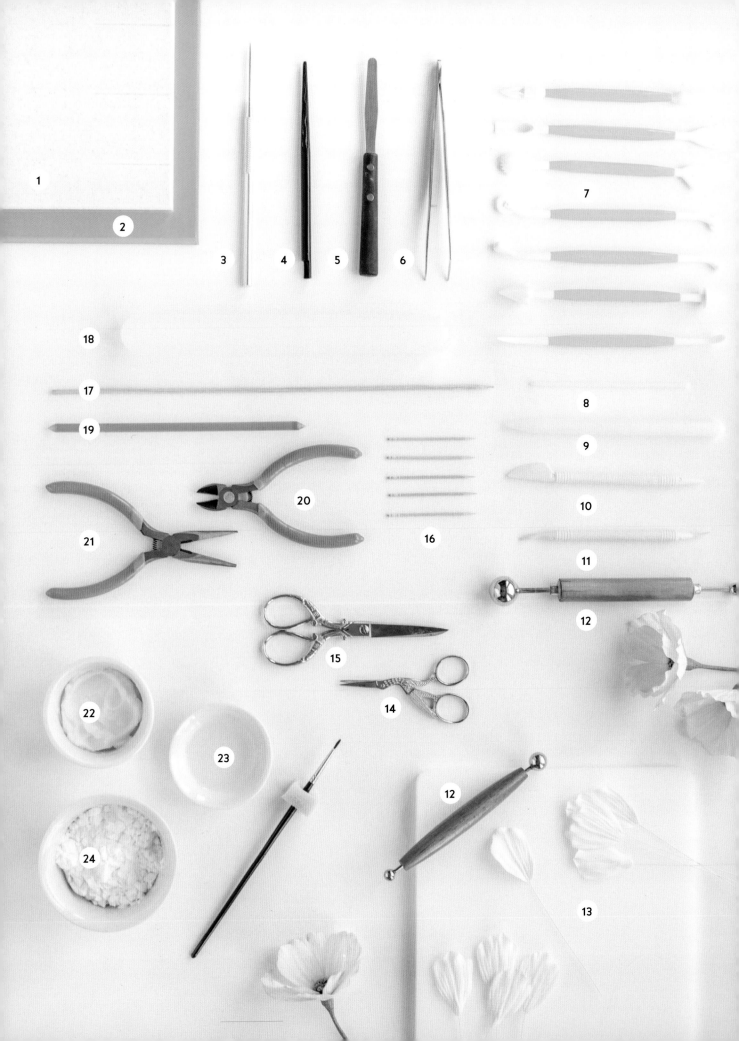

ESSENTIAL TOOL KIT

1 Groove board, a non-stick sugarcraft multi groove veining board with holes for Mexican hat flower backs, with a smooth rolling surface on the reverse side

2 Petal protector or acetate sheet to keep rolled paste and cut petals from drying too quickly

3 Needle tool

4 JEM veining tool

5 Mini palette knife

6 Tweezers

7 Set of sugarcraft modeling tools

8 Mini Celpin

9 Celpin

10 Knife/scriber tool

11 Dresden tool

12 Metal ball tools in a variety of sizes

13 Foam petal pad

14 Small embroidery scissors, both straight and curved

15 Sharp scissors

16 Toothpicks (or cocktails sticks)

17 Wooden skewers

18 Non-stick small rolling pin

19 Mini rolling pin

20 Wire cutters

21 Pliers, for making hooks in wires, and to aid in flower arranging

22 Vegetable shortening (white vegetable fat)

23 Sugar glue and a small brush

24 Cornstarch (cornflour)

SPECIALIZED TOOLS AND SUPPLIES

1 Styrofoam balls in a variety of sizes

2 Flat and round paintbrushes for dusting and detail work

3 Metal leaf cutters (hydrangea leaves)

4 Leaf cutter and leaf veiner sets (cherry blossom leaves)

5 Metal petal and flower cutters (sweet peas)

6 Petal dust

7 Gel food colors

8 Flat paintbrushes for dusting

9 Detail paintbrush

10 Silicone leaf veiners

11 Metal petal cutters (hydrangea)

12 Plastic half sphere molds and formers in a variety of sizes

13 Hanging rack

14 Size guide for gumpaste and modeling paste

15 Egg crate foam for drying petals and leaves

16 Silicone petal veiners

17 Polyester outdoor thread

18 Cotton sewing thread

19 Styrofoam buds (Celbuds)

20 "Pollen" created with unflavored gelatin mixed with petal dust (see Getting Started).

21 Floral tape

22 Silcone leaf veiners (all-purpose)

23 Metal petal cutters (small rose petals)

24 Metal petal cutters (dahlia)

25 Metal petal cutters (freesia)

26 Stamens

27 Florist wire

GUMPASTE AND COLORING

Gumpaste is a pliable dough usually made with sugars, egg whites or oils, vegetable shortening and a gum agent, which makes the paste elastic and allows it to be rolled very thin. This makes it ideal for flower making, and it can also be used for modeling, ribbons and other fine detail work. There are a lot of wonderful pastes available; from homemade to ready-to-use commercial brands. As with other aspects of sugarcraft, gumpaste is sensitive to different weather conditions and environments, so it's best to try a variety of pastes to find what will work best for you. When working, keep cornstarch (cornflour) handy to dab on hands if the paste feels sticky, and a bit of vegetable shortening on fingertips if the paste feels dry.

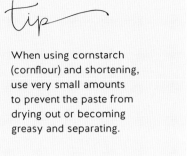

tip

When using cornstarch (cornflour) and shortening, use very small amounts to prevent the paste from drying out or becoming greasy and separating.

TYLOSE GUMPASTE

The gumpaste recipe I have used for years was created by the fabulous Chef Nicholas Lodge, and he has graciously given me permission to share it here. It's quick and easy to make, smooth and elastic, and dries beautifully.

- 125g fresh or pasteurized egg whites
- 725g + 100g powdered sugar/icing sugar
- 30g (27g*) tylose powder
- 20g vegetable shortening (Crisco)

1. Place egg whites in a mixer fitted with the flat paddle attachment. Turn mixer on high speed for a few seconds to break up the egg whites.

2. Turn mixer to the lowest speed; slowly add the 725g of powdered sugar to make soft consistency royal icing.

3. Turn up the speed to medium-high for about 2 minutes.

4. Make sure the mixture is at the soft-peak stage. It should look like shiny meringue with the peaks falling over. If coloring the entire batch, add the gel color at this stage, making it a shade darker than desired.

5. Scrape down the bowl and turn the mixer to the slow setting and sprinkle the tylose powder in over a 5 second time period. Turn the speed up to the high setting for a few seconds to thicken the mixture.

6. Scrape mixture out of the bowl onto a work surface sprinkled with some of the reserved 100g of powdered sugar. Place shortening on your hands and knead the paste, adding enough of the reserved powdered sugar to form soft but not sticky dough. Check by pinching with your fingers, they should come away clean.

7. Wrap the finished paste in cling-wrap and then in a zip-top bag. Place the bag in a second zip-top bag, and keep it well sealed. Place in the refrigerator and mature for 24 hours if possible.

8. When ready to use, allow the paste to come to room temperature. Cut off a small amount and knead a little vegetable shortening into the paste. If coloring at this stage, knead the gel color into the paste until the desired shade is achieved.

9. When not in use, store the paste in the refrigerator. The paste will keep under refrigeration for approximately 6 months. You can keep the paste longer by freezing it.

10. Less tylose can be used if you do not want the gumpaste to dry as fast, or if making dark colors that typically dry out the gumpaste (black, dark greens, purples).

NOTE: Certain brands of tylose powder are a stronger blend than others. Try using less in the recipe if using a different brand than ISAC Tylose Powder.

COLORING

To color gumpaste add gel color with a toothpick and knead the paste until the color is blended completely. Remember that the color will deepen a bit while it is resting, but will get lighter as the paste dries.

To create pretty pastels, make a small amount of the desired color but in a dark shade. Once this base color is created, add white paste to it until the desired lighter shade is achieved. I find this quicker and easier than trying to create the correct shade with a larger ball of paste.

For greens, we use the following shades most frequently to keep our arrangements looking pretty and fresh. Begin by making a base color of moss green (Wilton Moss Green) or avocado green (Americolor Avocado). We like both colors as is for some of our leaves. The second shade is created by adding a bit of yellow (Americolor Lemon Yellow) to the base green for a soft color that works easily with pastels and is nice for small leaves and calyxes. The third shade is created by adding a bit of dark green (Americolor Forest Green) to the original base color to create a deeper color for darker leaves. These three shades can cover a wide variety of greenery and are easy to replicate with other brands of gel color in similar shades.

THE
Formula

The formula at Petalsweet is quite simple, and more importantly, it always works!

THE FORMULA = GREEN + WHITE + PASTELS

I wish I could say I studied color theory with great focus and enthusiasm, but the Petalsweet formula actually came together because of three simple things… my long-time obsession with green, how I love the freshness of green and white together, and from a moment of major procrastination when making a wedding cake.

Early in my career, I didn't leave myself much time to make and finish peonies and roses for a cake, so I quickly made them in a very pale base color of pink, and when dry, added a bit more color just to the edges of the petals with petal dust. The result was a collection of pastel flowers I fell in love with, not only for their delicate finish, but also for how quickly they came together. It was the perfect combination of delicate prettiness mixed with practicality for my production schedule.

I started reproducing my favorite greens in hydrangea, buds and leaves, and I knew many of the pastel flowers would also look beautiful in white. The final part of the equation was creating little filler blossoms to help solve the problem of gaps between flowers in an arrangement. I created them in white because they were super easy to mix with everything else!

All of these elements came together as the Petalsweet formula.

The look is simple to reproduce, and is consistently modern, fresh and pretty. It's happily become our signature look, and I hope you are inspired to give it a try!

GETTING STARTED

Before you begin making beautiful flowers and arrangements for your cakes, please take a moment to review the general information and techniques listed here, as you will be using them frequently in your flower making.

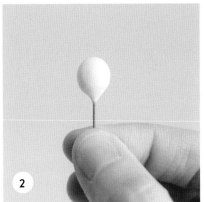

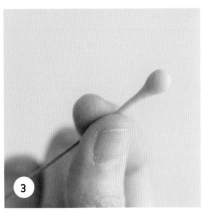

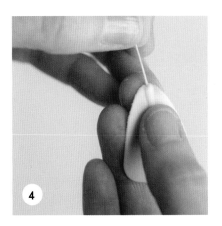

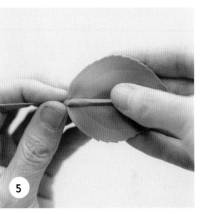

HOOKING WIRES

Create small hooks in your wires to help pieces of paste to stick to the ends of the wires **(1)**. Making the perfect hooked wires takes just a few steps. For an open hook, grab the top of the wire with pliers and bend the top over without closing. To make a closed hook, squeeze the open hook closed with the pliers.

ATTACHING PASTE TO A WIRE

To attach a ball of paste to a wire, dab a small amount of sugar glue on the hook and wipe off the excess so it is just damp. Insert the hook into the center of the ball of paste. Pinch a small amount of paste out of the bottom of the ball, turning the wire and pinching until the extra paste below the ball is quite thin. Hold on to the paste with your fingers and twist the wire quickly to break off the extra paste. For a longer bud shape, begin the same way, inserting the hook into the widest part of the bud. Gently roll the paste back and forth between your fingers to taper the paste down the wire until the desired length is reached. Twist the wire to break off any extra paste and gently roll the end between your fingers to smooth **(2 and 3)**.

WIRING PETALS & LEAVES

There are a lot of different methods for wiring petals and leaves. I prefer using the groove board because you can create a lot of petals and leaves quickly, neatly and consistently. Once you have rolled your paste and cut your petal or leaf shape, dip your wire end into sugar glue and wipe off the excess so it is just damp. Hold the base of the petal or leaf between your thumb and finger with the groove facing up towards you. Gently insert the wire into the groove to get it started, and then continue a bit at a time, using your thumb over the top to feel the wire **(4)**. Once the wire is in the groove, gently pinch where the paste and wire come together to secure **(5)**. If this does not work for you, lay the petal or leaf on the foam pad with the groove side up and the base at the edge of the pad. Place your finger gently on the groove, and insert the wire a bit at a time. Secure the wire as described above.

USING FLORAL TAPE

Floral tape comes in a variety of colors and widths. A nice moss green or yellow-green color will probably be the most useful, but you may also want to use white tape if you are making an all white or light colored arrangement or it's difficult to hide the green stems. You can also dust floral tape to create custom colors as desired. Half-width tape is what we use most frequently, but use what you are most comfortable handling. Try to use as little tape as possible to avoid bulkiness on stems. There are some wonderful tape cutters available that easily cut tape into halves, thirds, and even fourths. To use the tape, cut it to the desired length and stretch it a bit to release the gums in the tape. Wrap the tape tightly and firmly to keep wired petals secure. To wrap down a stem, hold the tape at a slight downward angle and turn the flower as you wrap tightly down the wire **(1)**.

BRUSHES & DUSTING

For best dusting results, I recommend a mix of both flat and round brushes. Flat, firm brushes are great in sizes ⅛in (3mm) up to ¾in (2cm) and are perfect for edging petals and leaves, and applying color in small or specific areas. Round, soft brushes ½in (1cm) up to 1in (2.5cm) are great for applying a soft blush of color and blending shades on petals, or adding color across large petals quickly.

Begin dusting your flowers with colors lightened with cornstarch (cornflour) or white petal dust, and use a light touch with your brush. You can always add and layer more color, but you can't take it away if you start heavy-handed. With pastel colored petals, simply edging them with a slightly darker shade makes the petals and finished flowers look airy and delicate without having to use much color. When possible, practice any new color combinations on extra dried pieces of paste. For leaves, we use most of our favorite green dusts full strength to create fresh, saturated color.

POLLEN

"Pollen" is used to dust the ends of stamens in some flowers, adding a realistic touch. It can be created with unflavored gelatin mixed with petal dust. Mix in the dust half a teaspoon at a time until the desired color is achieved **(2 and 3)**.

STEAMING & GLAZING

Gently steam your flowers and leaves to set the dust colors and prevent color from transferring to your cake surfaces. The dryness of the dust will disappear, and colors will blend together a bit like watercolor. Dust colors will deepen a bit after steaming, so keep this in mind when creating dust shades for your flowers. Hold flowers at least 6in (15cm) away from the steam and move them around constantly to make sure no part of the flower absorbs too much moisture **(4)**. Steam for a few seconds at a time, just until the flower no longer looks dry, but not so long that it looks shiny. Steaming too long can cause flowers to become soft and then wilt or fall apart. Allow steamed flowers and leaves to dry completely before using.

Confectioner's glaze and leaf glaze are great for giving your leaves a shiny finish. Use the glaze in very small quantities, and apply it with a brush in a very thin layer on leaves that have been dusted, steamed and are completely dry **(5)**. The glaze can also be thinned to a 50/50 ratio with alcohol or glaze thinner if you want less shine. Drying time varies in different weather conditions, with longer drying time occurring in more humid and wet weather. There are several versions of glaze on the market, and some may require more than one coat to get the desired finish. If a matte or velvet finish is desired for leaves, then steaming will suffice.

Hydrangea

I have included hydrangea here in the beginning of the book because they are one of the essentials used in many of our cake designs. Green hydrangea are our favorite because they add freshness to arrangements and make the pastel flower colors pop, but try them in purple, blue, pink, and white too! When making them, let them dry two ways – hanging from a rack so the shape is more closed, and face up in a cupped former so the flower remains more open. The closed hydrangea flowers nestle closely together, which is one of my secrets to creating tight arrangements.

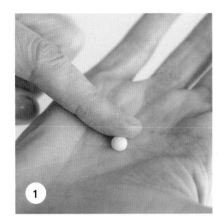

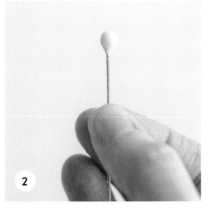

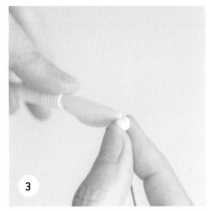

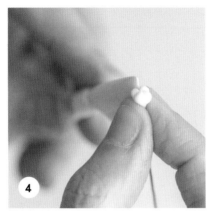

SPECIFICS YOU WILL NEED

....

- Hydrangea flower cutter (Cakes by Design)
- Hydrangea flower single-sided veiner (Cakes by Design)
- Hydrangea leaf cutter (Cakes by Design)
- Hydrangea leaf single-sided veiner (Cakes by Design)
- 26g green wire
- Knife tool
- Shallow cupped formers for flowers
- Hanging rack
- Egg crate foam
- Kiwi green petal dust
- Moss green petal dust
- Daffodil petal dust
- Magenta pink petal dust
- Confectioner's glaze (leaf glaze)
- White paste
- Hydrangea green paste (Americolor Avocado and Lemon Yellow)
- Leaf paste (Wilton Moss Green and Americolor Avocado)

MAKE THE CENTERS

1. Roll a tiny ³⁄₁₆in (4mm) ball of white paste until it is smooth.

2. Attach neatly to 26g green hooked wire (see Getting Started).

3. Use a knife tool to make an indentation across the middle of the paste to create two halves.

4. Use the knife tool to make two more indentations dividing the halves into half again.

5. Make a center for each hydrangea flower you will be creating. Let them dry completely.

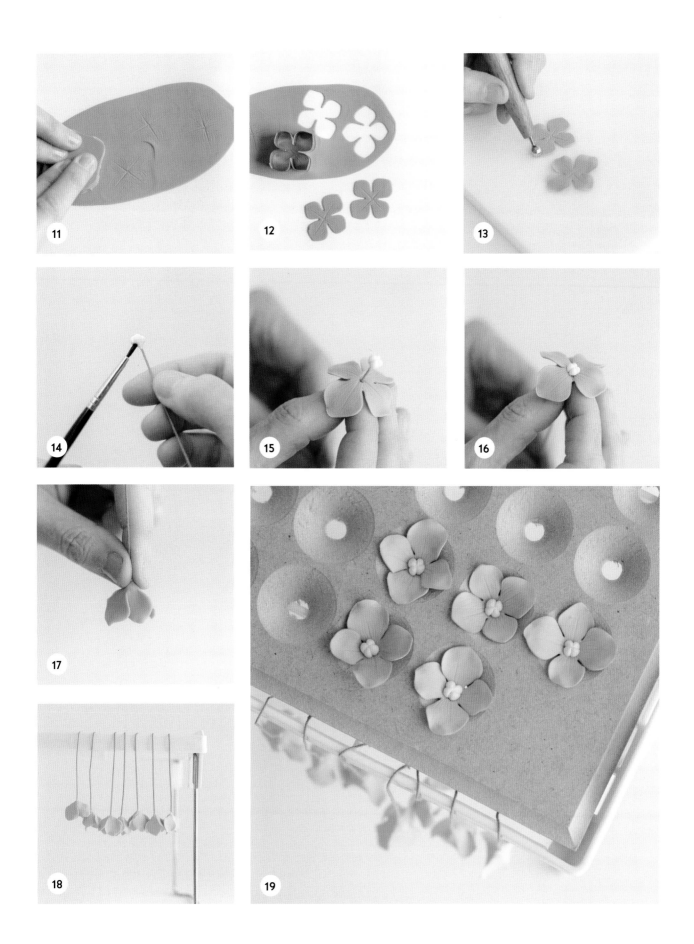

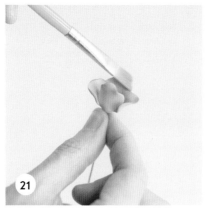

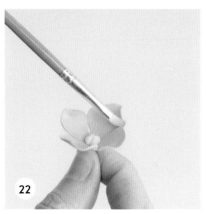

tip

When gathering together hydrangea flowers and buds into a bouquet, allow the pieces to all be at slightly different heights. This will make them look more natural.

DUST THE BUDS AND FLOWERS

20. Dust a kiwi green color over the entire bud.

21. Dust a kiwi green on the hydrangea flowers, working from the outer edges in towards the center, avoiding getting color on the white centers.

22. Add a bit of pink dust on random edges of the flowers if desired.

23. The closed hydrangea flowers fit together more tightly, but the open petals add some charm and dimension.

MAKE THE LEAVES

24. Roll the green leaf paste until moderately thin, to about 1/16in (2mm), on the groove board.

25. Press the paste evenly with the hydrangea leaf veiner, centering it over the groove.

26. Move the paste to a cutting surface and cut a hydrangea leaf.

27. Dip the end of a 26g green wire into sugar glue. Insert it about 1in (2.5cm) into the groove on the back of the leaf (see Getting Started).

28. Pinch the paste where the wire enters the leaf to secure it to the wire.

29. On a foam pad, thin the edges of the reverse side of the leaf with a ball tool. Repeat with heavier pressure on the edges to add movement.

30. Lay the leaf right-side up on a piece of foam to dry completely.

31. Dust the topside of the leaf with moss green dust, leaving the underside untouched.

32. Add a bit of yellow dust and a kiwi green dust in small random splotches on the leaf.

33. Dust a tiny bit of pink on random parts of the edge of the leaf.

34. Steam the leaf for a few seconds to set the colors and let it dry (see Getting Started).

35. If desired, dab the topside of the leaf with a thin coat of confectioner's glaze or leaf glaze to create a nice shine. Let the leaves dry completely before using.

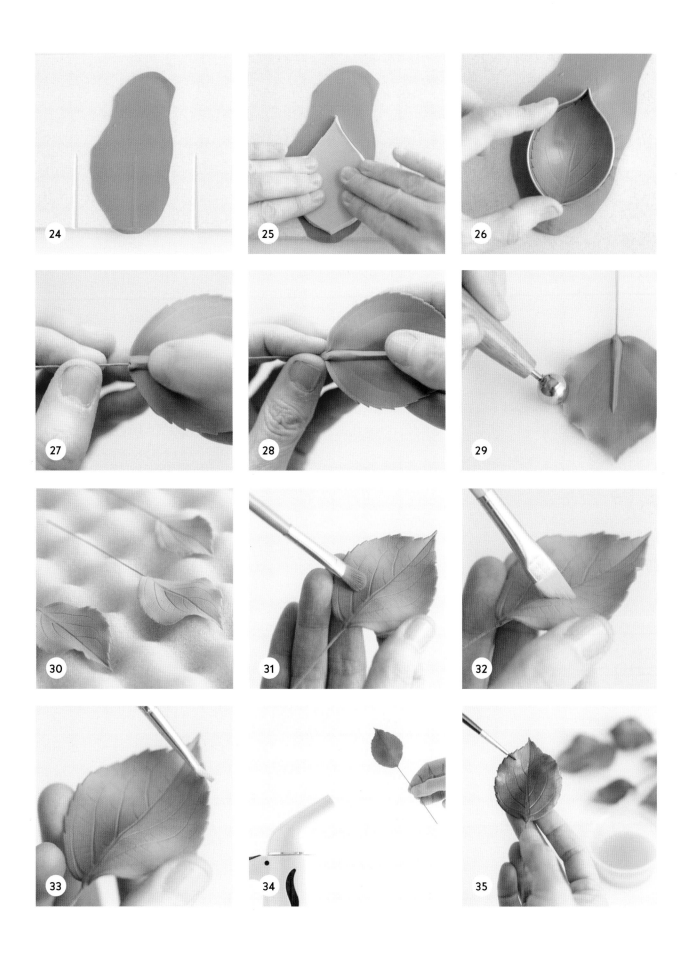

ADDITIONAL LEAVES

Beautiful leaves are great for framing, finishing and bringing life to flowers and arrangements. Here are the leaves I use most frequently. Don't worry about having the exact leaves to match all your flowers, I keep a supply of hydrangea, rose and peony leaves and some greenery on hand, and then I'll make a specific leaf just when I need it. Follow the rolling, cutting and wiring instructions for the hydrangea leaves, but press the wired leaves between the silicone veiners before drying and finishing.

RANUNCULUS LEAVES (1)

- Moss green paste/26g wire
- Ranunculus leaf cutter (Scott Woolley)
- Silicone rose leaf veiner (SK Great Impressions)
- Moss green petal dust
- Steam and glaze to finish

LILAC LEAVES (2)

- Avocado green paste/26g wire
- 1⅜ x 1¾in (3.5 x 4.5cm) rose petal cutter
- Multi-purpose veiner (Sunflower Sugar Art)
- Kiwi green petal dust
- Steam and glaze to finish

CAMELLIA LEAVES (3)

- Moss and forest green paste/26g wire
- Use cutting wheel to cut leaf shape (see template*)
- Silicone rose leaf veiner (SK Great Impressions)
- Moss green petal dust
- Steam and glaze to finish

SWEET PEA LEAVES (4)

- Avocado green paste/28g wire
- Mistletoe cutters (Scott Woolley)
- Multi-purpose veiner (Sunflower Sugar Art)
- Kiwi green petal dust
- Steam and glaze to finish

GREENERY (5)

- Moss green paste/28g wire
- Use cutting wheel to cut leaf shapes (see templates*)
- Multi-purpose leaf mat (First Impressions Molds)
- Moss green petal dust
- Steam to finish

MAGNOLIA LEAVES (6)

- Moss green (top) and orange-brown paste (underside) rolled together over grooved board/24g wire
- Use cutting wheel to cut leaf shape (see template*)
- Magnolia leaf veiner (First Impressions Molds)
- Moss green petal dust
- Steam to finish

CHERRY & APPLE BLOSSOM LEAVES (7)

- Moss green paste/28g wire for cherry blossom
- Avocado green paste/28g for apple blossom
- Small multi-purpose leaf cutter and veiner (Scott Woolley)
- Moss green petal dust for cherry blossom
- Kiwi green petal dust for apple blossom
- Steam and glaze to finish

DAHLIA LEAVES (8)

- Moss green and yellow paste/26g wire
- Hydrangea leaf cutter (Scott Woolley)
- Use small scissors to cut v-shaped snips out of leaf edges
- Silicone leaf veiner (First Impressions Molds – gardenia)
- Moss green and kiwi green petal dust
- Steam and glaze to finish

ROSE LEAVES (9)

- Moss green paste/26g wire
- Rose leaf cutters in large and small (Scott Woolley)
- Silicone rose leaf veiner (SK Great Impressions)
- Moss green petal dust on leaves
- Holly petal dust in center vein and on leaf edges
- Steam and glaze to finish

PEONY LEAVES (10)

- Moss and forest green paste/26g wire
- Use cutting wheel to cut leaf shapes (see templates*)
- Peony leaf veiner (Sunflower Sugar Art)
- Moss green and holly petal dust
- Steam and glaze to finish

Filler Flowers

BUDS AND LEAVES

Signature favorites at Petalsweet, these little pulled blossoms
and all-purpose buds go with just about everything! The
flowers are most versatile made in white with pale yellow
centers, but can easily be made in any color you need
to coordinate with other flowers in a design.

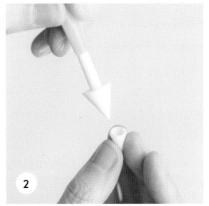

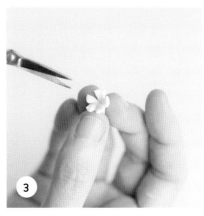

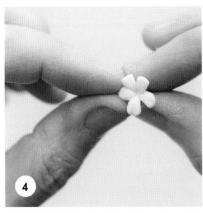

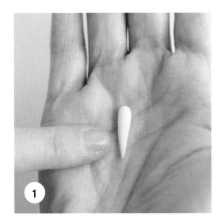

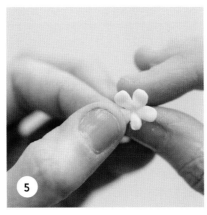

SPECIFICS YOU WILL NEED

- Cone tool
- Knife tool
- Small scissors
- 26g green wire
- 28g green wire
- 30g green wire
- 22g green wire
- Kiwi green petal dust
- Moss green petal dust
- Small amount of pale yellow soft royal icing (Americolor Lemon Yellow)
- Small piping cone (bag)
- White paste
- Green paste (Wilton Moss Green)

MAKE THE FLOWERS

1. Roll a small ¼in (5mm) narrow cone of white paste, 1in (2.5cm) long.

2. Open the top with the cone tool, creating a ¼in (5mm) deep hole.

3. Using scissors, cut into the rim of the opening five times to create the petals.

4. Using your fingers, gently press the square corners of the petals to round them.

5. Flatten the petals firmly between your thumb and finger.

6. Turn the flower upside down on a foam pad and cup the underside of each petal by gently pressing with a small ball tool. Continue to step 7.

7. Slide a hooked 26g wire down through the center of the flower, just until the hook disappears out of sight.

8. Gently roll the base of the flower between your fingers to attach it neatly to the wire. Set in styrofoam to let it dry completely.

9. Color a small amount of soft royal icing pale yellow and spoon into a piping cone. Snip a tiny tip off the point with scissors. Pipe the centers of the flowers, filling the tiny center hole with icing and hiding the tops of the wires. Allow to dry completely before using.

MAKE THE FILLER FLOWER BUDS

10. Roll a tiny ³⁄₁₆in (4mm) ball of white paste until smooth, and attach neatly to a hooked 28g wire (see Getting Started).

11. Use a knife tool to make three indentations evenly around the top of the bud. Let it dry. Dust a tiny amount of kiwi green color on the base of the bud to finish, and steam to set the color (see Getting Started).

MAKE THE LEAVES

12. Roll a tiny ³⁄₁₆in (4mm) ball of green paste into a cone and attach it to a hooked 30g wire, with the pointed end at the top. Flatten firmly between your thumb and finger.

13. Lay the leaf on a foam pad and press on both sides of the wire with your fingertips, creating a center vein and the sides of the leaf.

14. Smooth and stretch the two sides with a ball tool to create the leaf shape. Pinch the leaf tip to finish. Let it dry completely.

15. Dust with moss green dust and finish with a tiny dab of confectioner's or leaf glaze for a bit of shine. Let the leaf dry before using.

MAKE THE ALL-PURPOSE BUDS

16. Roll a ½in (1cm) ball of white paste into a chunky cone shape, and attach to a 22g hooked wire.

17. Use a knife tool to create three indentations from the base of the bud to the tip, evenly spaced around the bud. Let it dry completely.

18. Dust the base of the bud and up through the indentations with kiwi green dust. Steam for a few seconds to set color and let dry before using. Make the buds in both green and white, and in a variety of small sizes.

THE Flowers

Anemone

Known for their delicate petals surrounding a dramatic black center, we love anemones in fresh white to mix with our favorite greenery. The petals are dried in a gently cupped former to create a flower shape that is easy to nestle next to others in an arrangement. For an alternative version, dry the petals flat to create an open anemone as shown below, and use them layered over the gap between other flowers, or cascading down the side of a cake.

SPECIFICS YOU WILL NEED

....

- Pollen mixture in black (see Getting Started)
- Waxed dental floss
- Small rose petal cutter, 1⅛ x 1⅜in (3 x 3.5cm) (Cakes by Design)
- Large rose petal cutter, 1⅜ x 1⅝in (3.5 x 4.3cm) (Cakes by Design)
- Rose petal veiner (SK Great Impressions)
- Black double-ended stamens (round tip or folded tip or flat tip)
- Shallow cupped former (apple tray)
- Floral tape (green)
- 20g green wire
- 30g white wire
- White paste
- Black paste (Americolor Super Black)

MAKE THE CENTER

1. Roll a small ⅜–½in (8mm–1cm) ball of black paste until smooth, and secure it to a hooked 20g wire (see Getting Started).

2. Gently press the base of the ball with your fingers to make it slightly v-shaped. Allow it to dry completely.

3. Apply sugar glue or leaf glaze to the entire ball and dip it in black pollen mixture. Tap off any excess. Let it dry before adding the stamens.

4. Bend 20 stamens in half over the middle of a 6in (15cm) 30g white wire. Secure the wire tightly underneath the stamens by twisting several times. Make four or five bunches of stamens depending on the fullness desired.

5. Attach the loose end of a piece of waxed dental floss around the flower stem, and then attach a stamen bunch around the anemone center, wrapping tightly three times with dental floss at the base of the flower center before adding the next bunch of stamens. Add the remaining bunches in the same way, securing each one tightly and spacing them around the center as evenly as possible.

6. Once all the stamen bunches are attached, cover the stamens completely with floral tape to make a single stem. Use your fingers to adjust the stamens as needed to make them look evenly spaced around the center.

MAKE THE PETALS

7. To make the small petals, roll white paste thinly on the groove board and cut a 1⅛ x 1⅜in (3 x 3.5cm) rose petal shape.

8. Dip a 30g white wire in sugar glue, insert it ½in (1cm) into the groove, and secure at the base (see Getting Started).

9. With a ball tool and working on the foam pad, thin petal edges and then lengthen the center of the petal with two or three strokes.

10. Press the wired petal in the veiner.

11. Working on the foam pad and on the reverse side of the petal, create some gentle movement on the petal edges using the ball tool – create gentle waves, not strong ruffles.

12. Place the petal front-side up in an apple tray or other gently cupped former to dry. Make five or six small petals per flower.

13. To make the large petals, start the petal in the same way up to securing the wire, using a 1⅜ x 1⅝in (3.5 x 4.3cm) rose petal cutter. This time, stretch and widen the petals using a few strokes with the ball tool. Press in the veiner, use the ball tool on the back side edges to create movement, and lay in the former to dry. Make six or seven large petals per flower.

14. The mix of small and larger petals will give the anemone flowers a natural look and some visual interest.

ASSEMBLE THE ANEMONE

15. Using half-width floral tape (see Getting Started), attach a small petal at the base of the stamens where the tape begins.

16. Continue taping all the small petals at the same height, spacing them evenly around the stamens.

17. Begin adding the large petals, attaching them directly below the layer of small petals.

18. Gently steam the anemone flower for a few seconds to finish (see Getting Started). Let it dry completely before using.

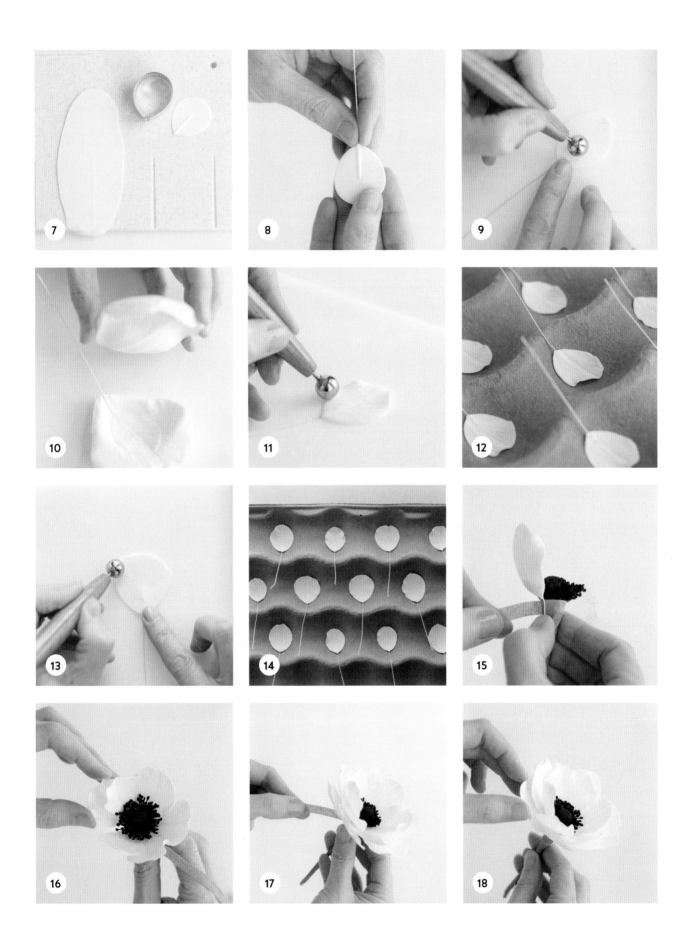

Camellia

A refreshing change from roses, camellias give you the look of a flower with many petals but without the fuss of creating perfect spirals. The colors range from white, to beautiful soft pinks, dark pink and red, and they are an iconic design symbol in the fashion house of Chanel. The instructions here make a beautiful open bloom, perfect to use as a stunning statement flower on top of small or individual cakes. If you wish to use them in an arrangement, simply hang them to dry so the finished camellias are shaped to fit well next to other flowers.

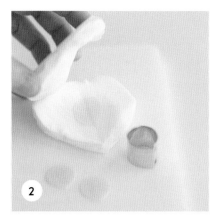

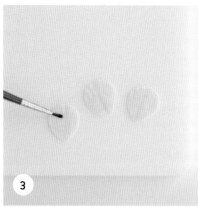

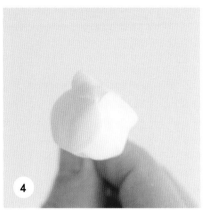

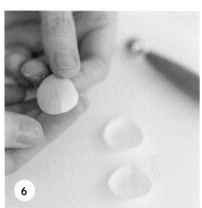

SPECIFICS YOU WILL NEED

....

- Celbud2 (20mm) for each bud and flower
- Rose petal cutters in five sizes: ½ x ⅝in (1 x 1.5cm), ¾ x ⅞in (2 x 2.3cm), ⅞ x 1in (2.3 x 2.5cm), 1⅛ x 1⅜in (3 x 3.5cm) and 1⅜ x 1⅝in (3.5 x 4.3cm) (Cakes by Design)
- Petal veiner (SK Great Impressions)
- Small scissors
- 20g green wire
- 22g green wire
- Cosmos pink petal dust
- Kiwi green petal dust
- Pale pink paste (Wilton Pink)
- Green paste (Wilton Moss Green and Americolor Lemon Yellow)

MAKE THE FLOWER

1. Glue a Celbud2 (20mm) to a 20g wire and let it dry.

2. Roll pale pink paste thinly, cut three ¾ x ⅞in (2 x 2.3cm) petals, thin the edges with a ball tool on a foam pad and press them in the petal veiner.

3. Apply sugar glue to the entire surface of all of the petals.

4. Attach the petals to the Celbud in a tight spiral, making sure to hide the tip of the styrofoam.

5. Smooth the petals down completely to form a tight bud.

6. Cut three ⅞ x 1in (2.3 x 2.5cm) petals. Thin the edges with a ball tool on a foam pad, and press them in the veiner. Then cup the insides of the petals with a ball tool on the foam pad. Gently pinch the center tip on the outer edge of each petal. Continue to step 7.

7. Apply sugar glue to the bottom half of the inside of the petals, and attach them so the petals are centered between the petals of the previous layer, and so they are slightly open from the center.

8. Prepare three more of the same size petals in the same way (as described in step 6), and attach them in between the petals of the previous layer and a bit more open.

tip

Look at photos of real camellias for inspiration on petal placement and flower fullness. Some camellias are very symmetrical while others are more loosely shaped.

9. Prepare six 1⅛ x 1⅜in (3 x 3.5cm) petals in the same way, and attach them around the center, spacing some evenly and some farther apart. These petals will overlap more. Repeat with a second set of six more petals in the same size.

10. Prepare six 1⅜ x 1⅝in (3.5 x 4.3cm) petals in the same way and attach them around the base of the flower.

11. To create notched petals, cut a small, rounded v-shape out of the center of the petal with scissors before pressing it in the veiner and cupping with a ball tool.

12. Prepare six 1⅛ x 1⅝in (3 x 4.3cm) notched petals as described in step 11, and attach them around the base of the flower.

13. To dry the camellia, place small pieces of tissue or foam between the layers of petals, to maintain the spacing as desired. The flower can be dried face up, resting gently on a flat piece of foam, or it can be hung to dry to create more of a closed shaped flower. Allow to dry completely.

14. To finish the camellia, remove all the tissue or foam. Dust the edges of all of the petals with pale pink dust and gently steam for a few seconds to set the color (see Getting Started). Let the flower dry before using.

MAKE THE BUD

15. Glue a Celbud2 (same size as for the flower center) to a 22g wire and let dry. Create the first three petals in the same way as the camellia flower, and attach in a tight spiral to cover the styrofoam.

16. Create three more ⅞ x 1in (2.3 x 2.5cm) petals lengthening each one a bit in the center with the ball tool before pressing it in the veiner. Apply sugar glue to the entire petal surface, and attach overlapping the first three petals, only slightly lower. Smooth with your fingers to attach cleanly to the bud.

17. To make the calyx, roll green paste thinly and cut six ½ x ⅝in (1 x 1.5cm) petals. Thin them with a ball tool and apply sugar glue to the surface of all of the petals. Attach in two layers of three petals each, placing the second layer so the petals are positioned in between those in the first layer, and lower down on the bud.

18. Dust the camellia bud with pale pink to match the flower, and kiwi green on the calyx. Gently steam for a few seconds to set the color. Allow to dry before using.

tip

The entire camellia flower can be created using the notched petals if desired.

CHERRY & APPLE Blossoms

What's not to love? Small, delicate and cute, cherry blossoms are adorable against pink, white and chocolate fondant. They are great on their own in small bouquets or used as single filler flowers in a mixed arrangement. Make lots of the tiny buds… they are quick and easy to make, and always a favorite!

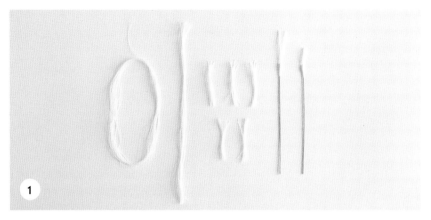

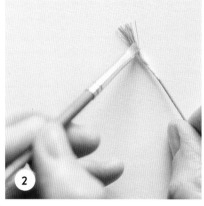

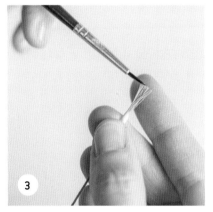

tip

If you are short on time, use pink thread for the stamens instead of white so you can skip the dusting. For a more formal variety of cherry blossom, use dark burgundy colored thread for the stamens.

SPECIFICS YOU WILL NEED

....

- Pollen mixture in yellow (see Getting Started)
- Celboard (groove board)
- Five-petal blossom cutter, 1⅛in (3cm) (Cakes by Design)
- Calyx cutter, ⅝in (1.5cm) (Orchard Products)
- Cotton thread (white)
- 26g green wire
- 28g green wire
- Egg crate foam
- Small scissors
- JEM veining tool
- Leaf shaping tool
- Floral tape (white)
- Magenta petal dust
- Cosmos pink petal dust
- Kiwi green petal dust
- Pale pink paste (Wilton Pink)
- Green paste (Americolor Avocado and Lemon Yellow)

MAKE THE CENTERS

1. Wrap white cotton thread in a loop 15 times around four of your fingers. Cut the loop once with scissors to make a long strip. Cut strip into 1in (2.5cm) sections. Use white half-width floral tape to attach a 1in (2.5cm) section to a green 26g wire (see Getting Started). Trim thread to ½in (1cm) length.

2. Dust the thread and base of the tape with magenta dust. Repeat with the remaining 1in (2.5cm) sections of thread.

3. Dab the ends of the sections of thread with sugar glue.

4. Dip the ends in yellow pollen mixture (see Getting Started) and allow them to dry completely.

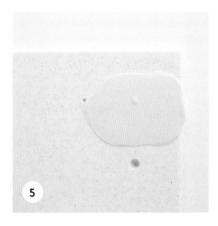

5

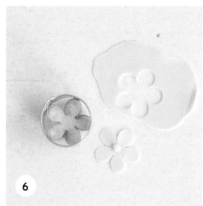

6

7

MAKE THE FIRST LAYER OF PETALS

5. Roll pale pink paste over the medium hole on a Celboard.

6. Pull off the paste, flip it over, move to flat surface, and cut the flower shape.

7. Using a ball tool on a foam pad, lengthen each petal by ¼in (5mm).

8. Using the JEM veining tool, vein each petal by rolling from the center to the outer edges.

9. Using scissors, cut a tiny ⅛in (3mm) slit in the center of each petal.

10. On a foam pad, thin the petal edges with a ball tool, and cup each of the petals twice with the wide end of a leaf shaping tool.

11. Apply a small amount of sugar glue in the center of the petal.

12. Slide one of the pre-made centers down through the middle of the petal, just until there is ⅛in (3mm) of tape showing in the center of the flower. Fold up the base of the petals around the center like tissue paper to hide the tape.

13. Gently roll the paste on the underside of the flower to attach it to the wire. Cut off the excess paste with scissors, leaving a ¼in (5mm) flower base.

14. Dry right-side up in egg crate foam to allow the first petal to remain slightly open. Allow the flower to dry completely before adding the second layer of petals.

MAKE THE SECOND LAYER OF PETALS

15. Roll pale pink paste to ⅟₁₆in (2mm) and cut the flower shape.

16. As with the first layer, lengthen and vein the petals, cut a slit in the top edge, ruffle and cup on a foam pad, and dab the center with a small amount of sugar glue.

17. Slide the petal up the wire and attach to the back of the first layer, positioning the petals so they are offset from the first layer. Hang to dry.

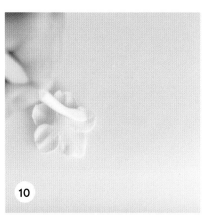

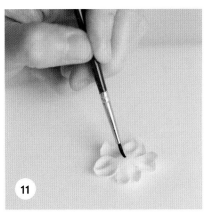

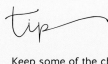

tip

Keep some of the cherry blossoms as single flowers without the second layer of petals. Having a mix of single and double flowers will look more natural in an arrangement.

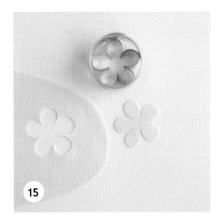

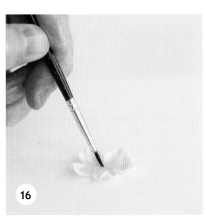

MAKE THE BUDS

18. Roll a small ball of pale pink paste around ⅜in (8mm) to ½in (1cm) in diameter and attach to a hooked 28g wire (see Getting Started). Let it dry completely.

19. Roll pale pink paste thinly to ⅟₁₆in (2mm) and cut the flower shape. Vein the petals and cup in the center of each each one with a ball tool. Apply sugar glue to all of the petals.

20. Slide the flower up the wire, and wrap the bud base with one petal at a time, smoothing them on the bud until all of the petals have been used. Smooth any square edges at the base of the bud with your fingers to create a round bud shape.

21. If desired, create a larger bud by adding a second layer of petals, but leaving some of the petals open.

tip

Apple blossoms can be created using the same techniques, substituting white paste for the flowers and buds, and leaving the thread white. To finish, dust the center of the flowers with kiwi green, and dust some of the flower edges and bud centers with a soft lilac color.

MAKE THE CALYX

22. Roll green paste thinly to ⅟₁₆in (2mm) and cut the calyx shapes.

23. Working with three at a time on a foam pad, widen the sections of the calyx with a small ball tool.

24. Pinch the tips of each section with your fingertips.

25. Dab a small amount of sugar glue in the center and attach a calyx to the base of all of the flowers and buds. Let them dry.

DUST THE BUDS AND BLOSSOMS

26. Dust the centers of the flowers with magenta, and the edges of the flowers with cosmos pink dust. Dust the buds all over with cosmos pink dust and then add a touch of magenta to the tips of the buds where the petals come together.

27. Dust the calyx and base of the flowers and buds with kiwi green dust. Gently steam to set the color (see Getting Started) and allow to dry completely before using.

tip

If you don't have time to make the calyxes, simply dust the base of the buds and flowers with a pretty yellow-green and steam to set the color before using.

Cosmos

The irresistible cosmos comes in a beautiful range of colors, from deep plum and magenta, to crisp white and the palest hint of blush. The delicate bright yellow center adds a fresh pop of color. The cosmos flower is a versatile wired flower that is easy to use in bunches as the focal flower in a design, or as a filler flower next to your other favorites.

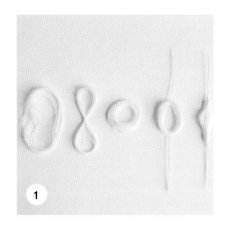

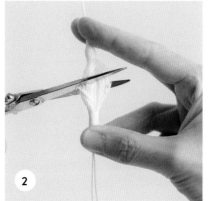

SPECIFICS YOU WILL NEED
....

- Pollen mixture in yellow (see Getting Started)
- Heavy-duty polyester thread in white
- Cosmos petal cutters, 1 x ⅝in (2.5 x 1.5cm) and 1 x 1½in (2.5 x 4cm) (Global Sugar Art)
- Cosmos petal veiner (Sunflower Sugar Art or Sugar Art Studio)
- 30g white wire
- 24g green wire
- Floral tape (white and green)
- Dresden tool
- Knife tool
- Extra blade/knife tools to use as formers (or similar)
- Aubergine petal dust
- Cosmos pink petal dust
- Kiwi green petal dust
- White paste
- Pale pink paste (Wilton Pink)

MAKE THE CENTER

1. Create a 5in (13cm) long loop of heavy-duty polyester thread by wrapping it around four spread fingers or a 5in (13cm) piece of cardboard. Twist the loop into a figure of eight and then fold over in half to create a smaller loop that is now twice as thick. Slide a 6in (15cm) length of 30g white wire through the center of the loop, fold the middle over the thread, and twist both ends of the wire tightly under the base of the thread. Repeat on the opposite side of the loop. Use half-width white floral tape to tape very tightly over the twisted wires and up onto the thread about ¼in (5mm) to keep the thread bunched together like the base of a "broom".

2. Cut the thread across the middle, creating two centers. Trim thread down to a ⅜in (8mm) length with an even, flat top.

3. Dust the thread and base of the tape with aubergine petal dust.

4. Using a small brush, dab the top of the thread with a little sugar glue or leaf glaze.

5. Dip the top of the flower center in yellow pollen mixture (see Getting Started), pressing firmly for even coverage.

6. Separate the threads a tiny bit with the end of a paintbrush to allow some of the dark threads to be seen. Allow the flower center to dry completely before using.

MAKE THE PETALS

7. Roll pale pink paste to ⅟₁₆in (2mm) thickness over the top half of a groove on the groove board.

8. Gently pull the paste from the groove and place on a smooth part of the board. Cut a petal shape using the 1 x ⅝in (2.5 x 1.5cm) petal cutter.

9. Dip a 4in (10cm) length of 30g white wire into sugar glue and insert it ½in (1cm) into the groove. Secure by gently pressing the paste neatly around the wire, maintaining the shape of the base of the petal (see Getting Started).

10. On the foam pad, thin the petal edges, and then gently lengthen the petal about ¼in (5mm) with a few upward strokes of a ball tool.

11. Press the petal in the veiner, with the grooved side facing down.

12. On the back side of the petal, lightly ruffle the top edge with a small ball tool.

13. Randomly press along the top edge of the petal three or four times with the small end of a Dresden tool to create a few ridges.

14. Dry the petal front-side down on the handle of a blade modeling tool, smoothing the bottom fifth of the petal over the handle to round it, and keeping the rest of the petal laying as flat as possible.

15. Make four of these to create the inner petals for the flower.

16. Repeat the petal-making process for the outer petals using a combination of the two petal cutters, but lay them all flat to dry rather than curving them round a modeling tool. Make four petals for the outer layer for a more botanically correct flower, or five petals (as pictured) for a fuller look.

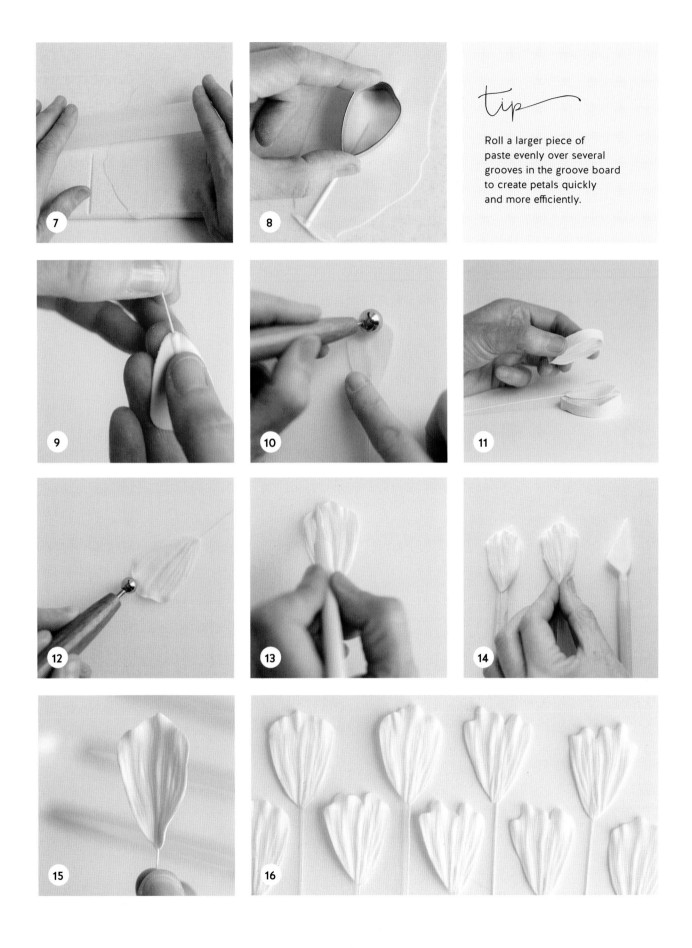

DUST AND ASSEMBLE THE COSMOS

17. Using a small flat brush, dust around the edges of the petals with a medium shade of cosmos pink dust, leaving the centers of the petals as is. If some of the underside of the flower will be seen, add some dust to the top half of the backs of the petals.

18. Using green half-width floral tape, attach the first inner petal to the center, with the cupped base hugging the thread and the base of the petal at the top of the white tape.

19. Tape the remaining three inner petals around the center at the same height, spacing them evenly.

20. Slide the first outer petal into position behind the inner petals, taping it in the gap between two petals. It should lay almost flat against the inner petals. If it is abruptly sticking out from the flower, drop the position slightly before taping so the petal layers are more flush.

21. Tape the remaining three or four petals around the flower in the same way, spacing them evenly. Wind the floral tape evenly down the length of the wires to create a single stem.

22. Gently steam the flower for 3 or 4 seconds to set the petal dust (see Getting Sarted). Allow it to dry before using.

MAKE THE BUDS

23. Roll a smooth ball of white paste around ⅜in (8mm) to ½in (1cm) in diameter. Attach neatly to a 24g hooked wire (see Getting Started).

24. Use a knife tool to make five indentations around the ball, pressing from top to bottom. Allow it to dry completely.

25. Dust the base of the bud with kiwi green and the tip of the bud with pale pink to match the flowers. Gently steam for a few seconds to set the petal dust. Allow it to dry before using.

Dahlia

Showstoppers, dahlias can easily steal the spotlight when used on their own, but can also be wonderful mixed with other flowers. Ours are made with individual petals, so it's easy to customize them with the time you have available. I've included two ways to make the dahlia center, one of which can also be used as a bud. With over forty species and too many colors to count, dahlias are extravagant and completely worth the work!

tip

To cut a daisy shape cleanly, press the cutter firmly into the paste, then turn it over and run your finger over each petal. To release the paste, gently push out each petal with the rounded end of a paintbrush.

SPECIFICS YOU WILL NEED

··

- ⅝in (1.5cm) styrofoam ball
- ¾in (2cm) styrofoam ball
- 20g green wire
- Dahlia petal cutters in three sizes: ½ x 1¼in (1 x 3.2cm), ⅝ x 1⅞in (1.5 x 4.7cm), ⅞ x 2¾in (2.3 x 7cm) (Cakes by Design)
- Twelve-petal daisy cutter in two sizes: 1¼in (3.2cm), 2½in (6.5cm) (Cakes by Design)
- Eight-petal daisy cutter for the flower calyx (optional), 1¾in (4.5cm) (Cakes by Design)
- Calyx cutter, 1in (2.5cm) (FMM)
- Dresden tool
- Small scissors
- Needle tool
- Cosmos pink petal dust
- Magenta pink petal dust
- Kiwi green petal dust
- Daffodil yellow petal dust
- Pale pink paste (Wilton Pink)
- Green paste (Wilton Moss Green and Americolor Avocado)

MAKE THE CENTER

1. Glue a ⅝in (1.5cm) styrofoam ball to a 20g wire. Let it dry.

2. Roll pale pink paste to ⅟₁₆in (2mm) and cut three 1¼in (3.2cm) twelve-petal daisy shapes.

3. Working with one daisy at a time on a foam pad, use a ball tool to thin and lengthen individual petals by about ¼in (5mm).

4. Cup each petal with a Dresden tool.

5. Cut a small "x" in the center of the daisy with scissors (this will help the petal break apart easily in the next step). Apply a small amount of sugar glue to the petals and the top of the styrofoam ball. Continue to step 6.

6. Slide the daisy up the wire and gently push the petals over the top of the ball so they overlap each other and hide the top of the ball. Prepare a second daisy in the same way and attach, trying to offset the petals so they lay in between each other. Don't worry that the base is not covered.

7. Repeat with a third daisy, but this time leave the petals a bit more open.

MAKE THE SMALL PETALS

8. Roll paste thinly to ⅟₁₆in (2mm) and cut 20 small dahlia petals. Keep them covered to prevent drying.

9. Working with five petals at a time, thin the edges with a ball tool on a foam pad. Using a needle tool, create veining down the center of each petal by marking once in the middle, and once each to the left and right following the shape of the petal.

10. Create movement on the edges of each petal with a ball tool, and pinch the tip of each petal.

11. Apply a small dot of sugar glue to the center bottom half of each petal.

12. Working with the bottom half of the petal, fold the right side into the center, and then close the left side of the petal over itself, rolling gently between your fingers to release.

13. Apply a small amount of sugar glue on the underside of the dahlia center and attach the five petals, evenly spaced around the center. Vary the heights of the petals from ¼in (5mm) to ½in (1cm) above the center. To create visual interest, place most of the petals facing towards the center, but attach a few turning sideways. Attach ten petals around the center, and then go back and fill in gaps with the remaining ten petals. Allow to dry for 30 minutes before adding the medium petals.

MAKE THE MEDIUM PETALS

14. Working with five petals at a time, make 20 medium petals in the same way as the small petals.

15. Attach to the flower in two layers of ten petals (attach ten petals first, and then fill in spaces between with the next ten petals). The flower at this stage can be used as a smaller version of a dahlia, especially if you need a variety of sizes for an arrangement. For added fullness, sneak in an additional layer of ten more petals before adding the large dahlia petals.

MAKE THE LARGE PETALS

16. Working with three petals at a time, make 14–16 large petals in the same way, but this time create five lines of veining on each petal with the needle tool. Fold and roll as with the small and medium petals, leaving the top half or two thirds of the petal open.

17. Again, attach the petals to the flower evenly spaced around the center but in two layers of seven or eight petals each. Hang the flower to dry, or dry face up, supporting the flower and petals with tissue or foam.

18. If the dahlia base will be seen, create a calyx by rolling green paste thinly to ⅟₁₆in (2mm). Cut a 1¾in (4.5cm) eight-petal daisy shape, vein it with the JEM tool, and attach it to the base of the flower with a little sugar glue. Allow to dry.

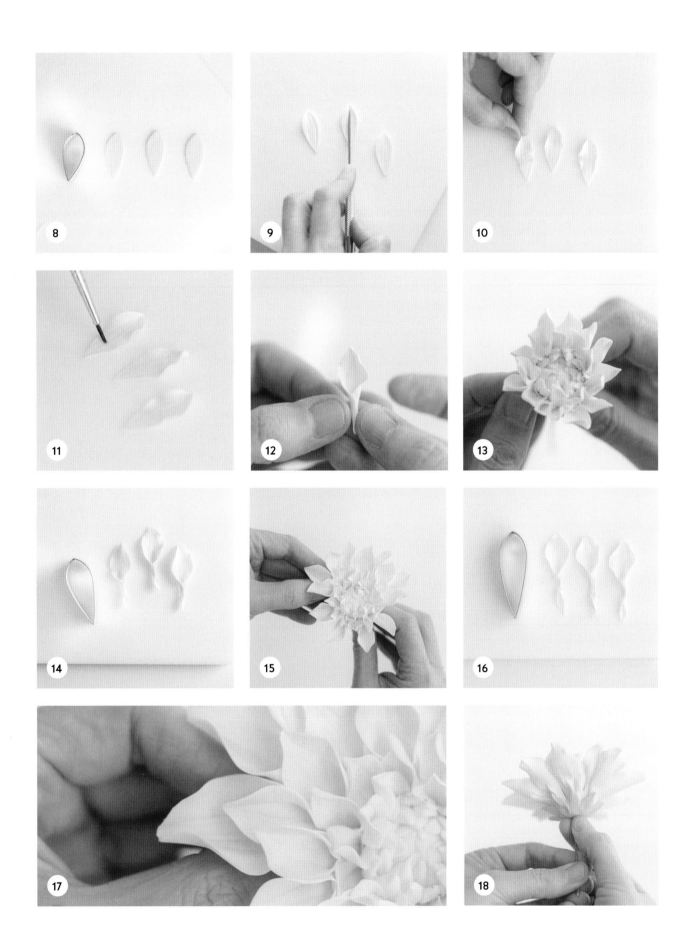

MAKE THE BUD

19. Glue a ¾in (2cm) styrofoam ball to a 20g wire and allow to dry.

20. Roll paste thinly to ¹⁄₁₆in (2mm) and cut four 2½in (6.5cm) twelve-petal daisy shapes. Keep them covered to prevent drying.

21. Working with one daisy at a time, thin and then lengthen the petals ¼in (5mm) on the foam pad with a ball tool.

22. Lightly score down the middle of each petal with a needle tool, working from the outer tip towards the center.

23. Apply sugar glue in the middle of each petal, fold one side over, and pinch the tip.

24. Apply sugar glue in the middle and at the base of the petals and attach around the ball, pulling the petals together to hide the top of the styrofoam ball.

25. Prepare and add the remaining three daisy shapes in the same way or until you reach the desired size of the bud. To make a smaller bud, reduce the number of daisy shapes to two or three.

26. To make a calyx, roll green paste thinly, and cut two 1in (2.5cm) calyx shapes. Stretch one of them with a ball tool to make it a bit longer and wider. Lightly vein with the JEM tool, and cup the segments with the wide end of the leaf shaping tool. Apply sugar glue all over the cupped surface of the smaller calyx. Turn the larger calyx over and apply glue only to the center.

27. Attach the small calyx to the base of the bud so the segments lie smooth against the bud. Attach the larger calyx so the cupped segments hang down away from the base of the bud. Allow to dry before dusting.

tip

To use the bud technique for the dahlia flower center, begin adding small or medium dahlia petals after you've layered two or three daisy shapes.

DUST THE DAHLIA AND BUD

28. Dust a pale shade of cosmos pink in the center of the flower.

29. Mix a small amount of magenta dust into the color used for the flower center. Dust in the openings of the first row of petals, and then on all of the tips and outer edges of the medium and large petals.

30. For the bud, dust all over with a pale shade of cosmos pink. Mix a small amount of magenta into the pale pink, and dust the tips of all of the petals. Dust kiwi green and a bit of yellow on the calyx. Gently steam the flower and bud for a few seconds to set the colors (see Getting Started) and allow to dry before using.

Freesia

With beautiful stems of funnel-shaped flowers and
delicate buds, freesia are a favorite for wedding
flowers and bouquets. They range in color from
white and yellow to pink, reds and purples, and when
taped together with their buds, add great texture
and visual interest to an arrangement. I love freesia
buds peeking out between other flowers. Freesia
can be used as a complete stem as shown, or you
can use the flowers on their own as pretty fillers.

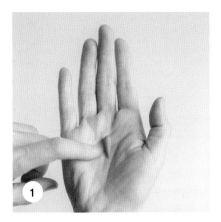

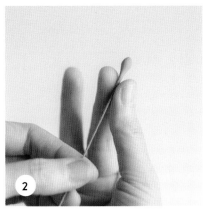

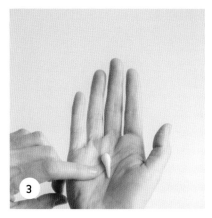

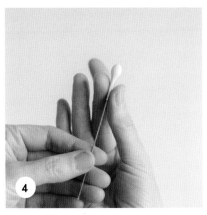

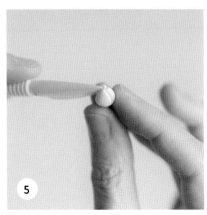

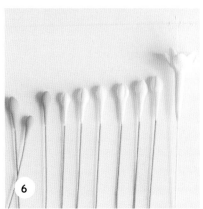

SPECIFICS YOU WILL NEED

· Freesia flower cutter (six-petal blossom cutter), 1⅛in (3cm) (Cakes by Design)
· Small round-tip stamens (white)
· Yellow gel color and small brush
· 28g green wire
· 26g green wire
· 26g white wire
· Knife tool
· Star tool
· Mini rolling pin
· Small scissors
· Floral tape (green and white)
· Hanging rack
· Kiwi green petal dust
· Moss green petal dust
· Daffodil yellow petal dust
· Cosmos pink petal dust
· White paste
· Green paste (Wilton Moss Green and Americolor Lemon Yellow)

MAKE THE GREEN BUDS

1. Roll a ¼in (5mm) ball of green paste until smooth, then roll the bottom half of it into a tapered narrow cone, leaving a bulbous tip. Make the bud ½in (1cm) to ¾in (2cm) in length.

2. Insert a hooked 28g wire into the base of the bud (see Getting Started) until the hook is in the middle of the widest part. Smooth the tapered end with your fingers to attach it cleanly to the wire. Let it dry. Make three green buds per freesia stem.

MAKE THE WHITE BUDS

3. Roll a ⅜in (8mm) ball of white paste and roll the bottom half into a narrow cone with a bulbous tip, as before. Make the bud ¾in (2cm) in length. Gently roll the top of the bud to taper it slightly.

4. Insert a hooked 28g wire to the base of the bud so that the hook is in the middle of the widest part. Attach it cleanly to the wire, as before.

5. Use a knife tool to make three indentations evenly spaced around the top of the bud. Let it dry completely.

6. Make the buds in graduated sizes ranging from ¾in (2cm) up to 1¼in (3.2cm), so the stem will look like it has buds that are increasing in size before blooming into flowers. Make five white buds per freesia stem.

MAKE THE CENTERS

7. Cut the tips off six small white round stamens. Attach half-width white floral tape to the top end of a 26g white wire, wrapping tightly round three times (see Getting Started). Attach the six stamens to the wire by taping over the bottom ½in (1cm) of the stamens tightly, and using as little tape as possible to avoid bulkiness.

8. Using a small paintbrush, dab yellow gel color on the tips of the stamens. Let them dry before using.

MAKE THE FLOWERS

9. Roll a ⅝in (1.5cm) ball of white paste.

10. Roll with your finger on one half of the ball to begin creating a cone shape, and press the bulbous end into your palm to begin a witch's hat.

11. Thin the paste that is the "brim" of the hat shape between your fingers to about ⅛in (3mm) leaving a ¾in (2cm) wide neck.

12. Using a mini rolling pin, roll the brim of the hat to ⅟₁₆in (2mm) keeping the thickness even from the neck out to the edge.

13. Center the cutter over the neck and cut the flower shape.

14. Use scissors to make a small cut to the base of the neck between each of the petals to separate them.

15. On a foam pad, working on the inside of the petals, use a ball tool to gently lengthen the petals with about three strokes, making them about one third longer. Do not overstretch the petals or they will not hold their shape in the final flower.

16. Press into the center of the flower with a star tool, creating a ¼in (5mm) opening.

17. Apply a small amount of glue to the taped center. Slide the wire down through the center of the flower until the tape is no longer visible.

18. Using your fingers, smooth the underside of the flower, maintaining a nice tapered shape, and securing it to the wire. Pinch off any excess paste and make sure to keep the bottom tip of the flower neat and clean. The final length of the neck should be between 1in (2.5cm) and 1¼in (3.2cm). Continue to step 19.

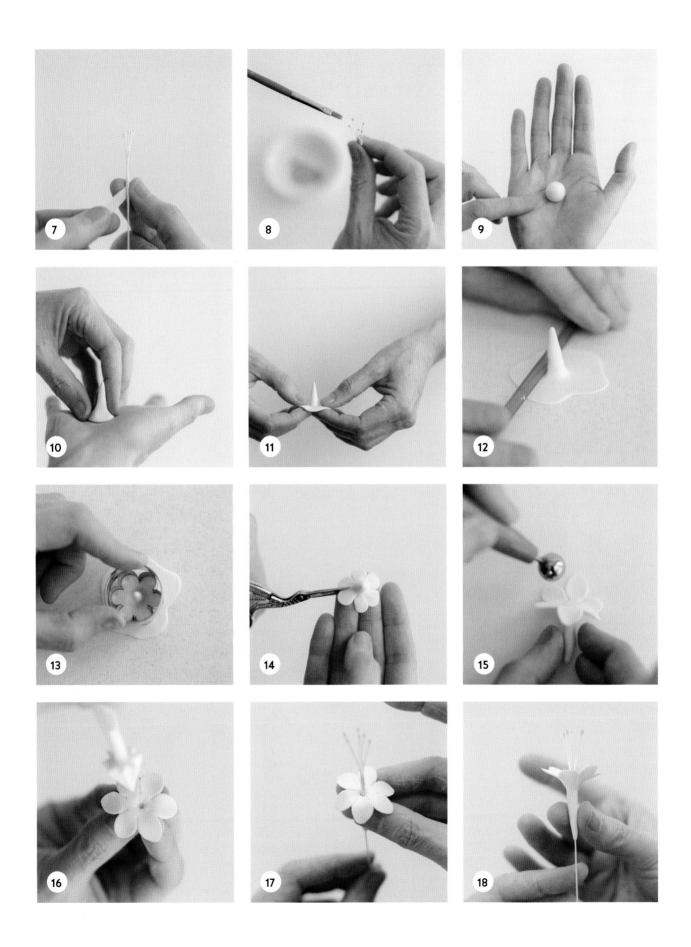

61

19. Hold the flower upside down and manipulate the petals with your fingers, shaping three of them so they are more closed around the stamens, and leaving the remaining three petals more open.

20. Hang the flower and let it dry completely. Make five flowers per freesia stem.

DUST THE BUDS AND FLOWERS

21. Dust kiwi green starting at the base of the flower going up about three quarters of the neck. Dust daffodil yellow over the top edge of the green dust and up underneath the flower petals.

22. Dust daffodil yellow in the flower center around the base of the stamens, and then cosmos pink on the top and bottom edges of the petals.

23. Dust the green buds all over with a mix of kiwi and moss green.

24. Dust the white buds in the same way as the flowers. Begin with kiwi green starting at the base of the buds going up about three quarters of the neck. Dust daffodil yellow over the top edge of the green dust and up underneath the widest part of the bud. Dust cosmos pink on the tips of the buds, leaving some white paste showing. Steam all of the flowers and buds for a few seconds (see Getting Started), and let them dry before using.

ASSEMBLE THE STEM

25. Lay out three green buds, five white buds and five flowers from the smallest to the largest size.

26. Using half-width green floral tape, attach the smallest green bud to the end of a 26g green wire, cut to 7in (18cm) length (see Getting Started).

27. Tape tightly down the wire to allow ¼in (5mm) of space before adding the larger size green bud. Tape neatly at the base of the bud, covering the wire.

28. Continue adding all of the green buds and white buds in the same way, making sure the spacing between them is even and consistent. They should all be lined up on the same side like "birds on a wire".

29. Attach the first flower slightly left of center, and the second flower slight right of center. This will allow the spacing at the base of the flowers to be consistent with the buds, allowing room for the open petals at the top of the flowers.

30. Tape the remaining three flowers by attaching the third flower in the center, the fourth flower slightly left again, and the final flower slightly right again. Tape all the way down the wires to create a single neat stem. Gently bend and shape the stem as desired.

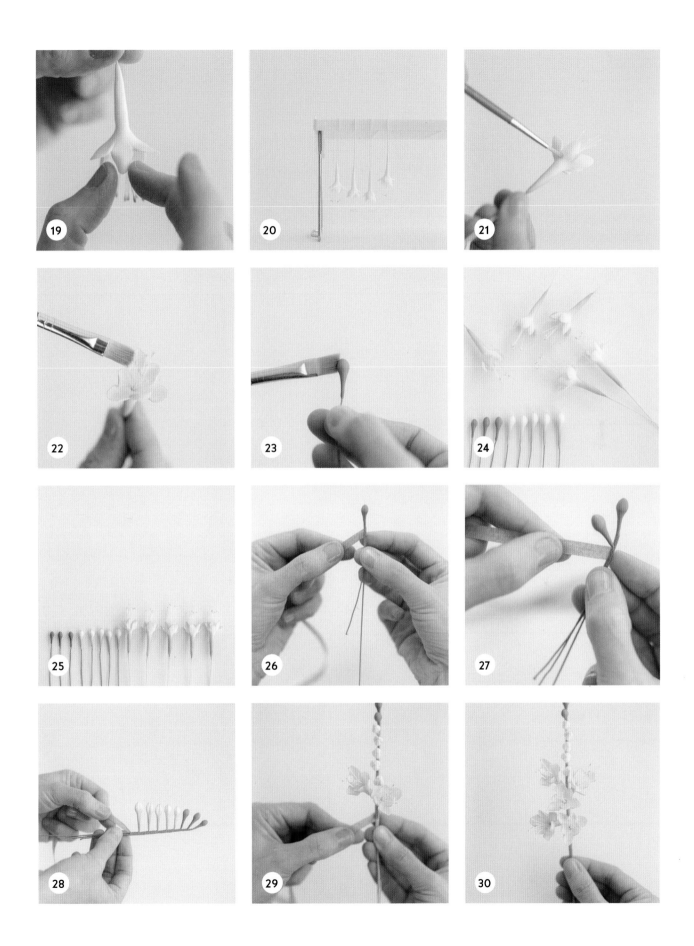

Lavender

Lavender stems are a great way to add height and a pop of color to your arrangements. A delicate addition to flowers perched on a cake ledge, they can also be laid on their side in a sweet bundle tied with ribbon. The most recognizable are the striking purple shades, but variations also include white and beautiful blues.

1

2

3

Work on five to seven stems at a time, moving from one to the next when you are adding new groups of petals. This will allow some drying time and reduce the risk of petals slipping down the wires.

4

SPECIFICS YOU WILL NEED

··

- Lavender petal cutter (six-petal flower cutter), ⅝in (1.5cm) (Orchard Products)
- Lavender calyx cutter (six-petal flower cutter), ⅜in (8mm) (Orchard Products)
- 26g green wire
- Hanging rack
- Lavender petal dust
- Royal blue petal dust
- Kiwi green petal dust
- Purple paste (Americolor Violet or Wilton Violet)
- Green paste (Americolor Avocado and Lemon Yellow)

MAKE THE STEM TIP

1. Using pliers, make a tiny closed hook in a 26g green wire cut to 7in (18cm) in length.

2. Roll a tiny ball of purple paste and attach it to the wire (see Getting Started), using only enough to neatly cover the hook. Let it dry for a few hours before using.

MAKE THE FIRST PETALS

3. Roll purple paste thinly to ⅛in (2mm) and keep it covered to prevent drying.

4. Cut and work with three or four lavender petal shapes at a time so the petals remain flexible while you work on them. Continue to step 5.

5. Dab a small amount of sugar glue on each petal.

6. Slide a petal up the wire and attach it around the stem tip, pressing gently to close the petal a little around the base.

7. Attach a second petal in the same way, trying to offset the tips so the petals don't sit directly on top of each other. For variety, make some stems with one petal over the stem tip, and some with two petals.

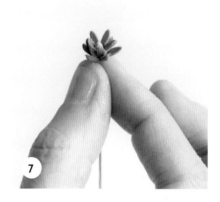
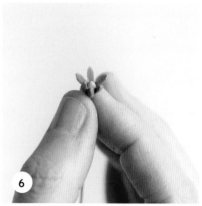

MAKE ADDITIONAL PETAL GROUPS

8. To create a new group of lavender petals, dab sugar glue on a petal and slide it up the wire, stopping about ⅜in (8mm) to ½in (1cm) below the previous group. Pinch the base of the petal, securing it to the wire. This is the "anchor" flower. Let this flower dry for at least 15 minutes before stacking additional petals below it.

9. Cut several more petals and apply glue in the centers. One at a time, slide them up the wire and attach to the anchor petal, trying to offset the tips so they don't line up with each other. For visual interest, vary the number of petals in each grouping by using between one and four petals per group.

10. Work on multiple stems at the same time to allow for sufficient drying time between groups of petals and individual stems. Let them hang on a rack during the process, and work all the way down the line before starting at the beginning again.

11. Use five or six groups of petals to create a lavender stem 2½–3in (6.5–7.5cm) in length.

MAKE THE CALYX (OPTIONAL)

12. Roll light green paste very thinly to ⅟₃₂in (1mm) and cut the calyx shape.

13. Using a small ball tool or tiny Celpin, widen the sections of the calyx, and then pinch the tips with your fingertips.

14. Dab a tiny amount of sugar glue in the center and slide the calyx up the wire to attach to the bottom petal of the lavender stem. Smooth with your fingertips to attach. Let the stems dry completely before dusting.

DUST THE STEMS

15. Dust all the petals with lavender dust.

16. Apply a few random spots of royal blue dust on the petals to add dimension.

17. Dust kiwi green at the base of each group of petals, and on the calyx. Steam to set the colors, and let the lavender stems dry before using.

18. Gently bend and shape the stems before using in an arrangement.

Lilac

Tiny lilac blossoms are a great filler flower! They come in a wonderful range of colors including soft pinks, blues and lavender shades, but I find them most beautiful and versatile in white and saturated purples. Make them in all stages of bloom, from buds to open flowers, and then mix them all together to create beautiful depth and texture.

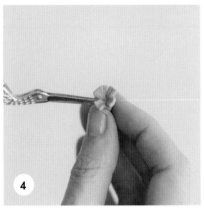

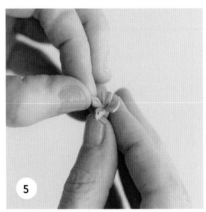

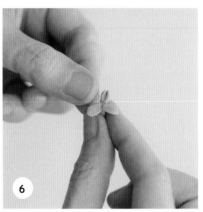

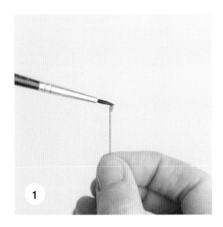

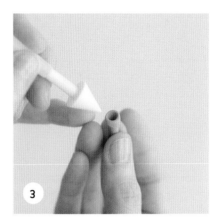

SPECIFICS YOU WILL NEED

- Pollen mixture in yellow (see Getting Started)
- 30g green wire
- Cone tool
- Small scissors
- Knife tool
- Leaf shaping tool
- Lilac petal dust
- Royal purple petal dust
- Amethyst petal dust
- Floral tape (green)
- Lilac paste (Americolor Violet and Electric Purple)

PREPARE THE CENTERS

1. Using pliers, create tiny closed hooks in 30g green wires cut to 3in (7.5cm) in length (see Getting Started). Using a brush, dab a tiny amount of sugar glue on the tips of the hooks.

2. Dip the tips of the hooks in yellow pollen mixture (see Getting Started) and let them dry completely before using them.

MAKE THE OPEN FLOWERS

3. Roll a tiny ¼in (5mm) ball of lilac paste into a narrow cone. Open the top with the cone tool.

4. Cut into the opening with scissors to create four petals.

5. Pinch the tips of the petals with your fingertips to create a point.

6. Flatten the petals firmly between your thumb and finger. Continue to step 7.

7. Holding the flower between your thumb and finger, press each petal with the wide end of the leaf shaping tool creating a ridge on the edge of the petal, and then slide the tool off your fingertip to lengthen the petal.

8. Press into the center of the flower with the cone tool, creating a small opening.

9. Slide a pre-made lilac center down through the middle of the flower until the pollen is tucked down in the opening. Smooth the base of the flower onto the wire to secure it neatly. Let it dry completely.

MAKE THE PARTIALLY OPENED FLOWERS

10. Start the partially opened lilac in the same way as the open flower including the step to flatten the petals between your thumb and finger. Then, on a foam pad, press the inside of each petal with a small ball tool to give them a cupped shape. Press the center of the flower with the tip of the cone tool, creating a small opening.

11. In the same way as the open flowers, slide a pre-made lilac center down through the middle of the flower until the pollen is tucked down in the opening. Smooth the base of the flower onto the wire to secure it neatly and let it dry completely.

MAKE THE BUDS

12. Roll a tiny ³⁄₁₆–¼in (4–5mm) ball of lilac paste into narrow cone shape with a bulbous tip.

13. Insert a hooked 30g green wire into the base (see Getting Started) until the hook is in the middle of the widest part of the bud. Smooth paste onto the wire to secure the bud.

14. Use the knife tool to make four indentations evenly around the top of the bud. Let it dry completely.

DUST THE BUDS AND FLOWERS

15. Dust the lilac buds all over with a mix of lilac and amethyst dust.

16. Dust all the lilac flowers from the outer petal edges towards the centers, avoiding the yellow centers if possible. Use several different colors of purple dust across all of the flowers. The soft mix of color will add a bit of dimension when the flowers are all taped together. Steam for a few seconds to set the colors (see Getting Started) and let the flowers dry before using.

GROUP THE LILACS

17. Using a single wrap of half-width floral tape (see Getting Started), simply tape together the buds and flowers in bunches of three. This can be three of the same (all buds or all open flowers) or three different stages of bloom (a bud, an open flower, and a closed flower). The more variety in the small bunches, the more natural the lilacs will look when grouped together in a larger bouquet.

18. Tape between three and five small bunches together into a larger bunch, and keep adding more flowers until the desired size is achieved.

Magnolia

Easily recognizable for their creamy white petals and lush green leaves, the magnolia is an elegant choice for a statement flower. The colors here make a flower that looks a bit more mature, but you can create a completely different look by dusting the center with a few of your favorite greens. Because the petals are clean and simple, the magnolia comes together quickly, and the two-tone leaves are the perfect final touch.

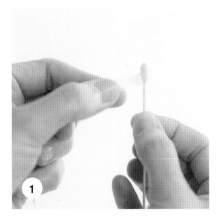

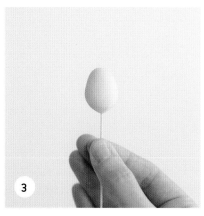

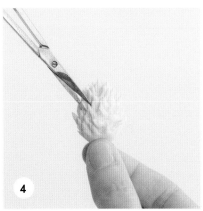

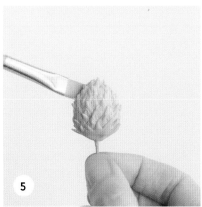

SPECIFICS YOU WILL NEED

···

- Magnolia petal cutters in two sizes: 2 x 2⅞in (5 x 7.3cm), 2⅞ x 3½in (7.3 x 9cm)
- 20g white wire
- 26g white wire
- Floral tape (white and green)
- Small scissors
- Apple tray (small petal former)
- Two 4½in (11.5cm) half sphere formers with a ¼in (5mm) hole in the center (large petal formers)
- Aluminum foil (optional)
- Kiwi green petal dust
- Daffodil yellow petal dust
- Orange petal dust
- Cocoa brown petal dust
- White paste
- Pale beige paste (Americolor Warm Brown)

MAKE THE CENTER

1. Using pliers, create a closed hook in a 20g white wire (see Getting Started) and then wrap it 12 times around with white half-width floral tape to create a small bud.

2. Roll a smooth ⅞in (2.3cm) ball of pale beige paste into an egg shape. Then use your fingers to press the base into a gently pointed v-shape.

3. Dab the taped bud with sugar glue and insert into the center of the paste. Secure the paste to the wire neatly at the base.

4. Using small scissors, snip into the paste, starting from the base and working your way to the tip. Make the cuts small and delicate, overlapping and layering them so they are not too uniform. Make a few small cuts into

the very top of the center as well. Use your fingers or a small tool to pull some of the bits of paste open to create more overall texture. Set aside and allow to dry completely for 24 hours before using.

5. Dust the bottom third of the magnolia center with pale green dust, and then add pale yellow dust over the remaining two thirds of the center.

6. Dust the top third with a pale mixture of orange and brown. Gently tap the wire on the edge of a table to knock off any excess dust. Steam the center to set the colors (see Getting Started) and let it dry before using. Additional color can be added if a darker center is desired. If more color is added, steam a second time before adding petals.

MAKE THE SMALL PETALS

7. Roll white paste on the groove board to ⅟₁₆in (2mm) thickness. Do not roll the paste too thinly (so it becomes see-through) as magnolias are known for their thicker and waxier petals.

8. Cut a small petal, rolling the paste with the base of the petal higher over the groove on the groove board so you end up with a groove on the reverse side of the petal that is only about ¾in (2cm) long. This is long enough to insert the wire, but most importantly, the finished magnolia petals won't have the shadow of the longer groove on the petals showing through from the reverse. The petals will just look creamy and elegant without giving away the "secret" of using the groove board.

9. Dip a 26g white wire into sugar glue and then insert it into the groove and secure neatly (see Getting Started).

10. Gently stretch the petal with a few light strokes of a rolling pin.

11. Working on the back of the petal, thin the edges with a ball tool on a foam pad.

12. Lay petals face up in the apple tray with gently cupped formers to dry completely. Make three small petals per flower.

MAKE THE LARGE PETALS

13. Roll paste on the groove board to ⅟₁₆in (2mm) thickness. Cut a large petal shape using a minimal groove on the reverse side (as in step 8). Dip a 26g white wire in sugar glue and insert into the groove, securing it neatly. On the reverse of the petal, thin edges with a ball tool on a foam pad.

14. Gently bend the wire 90 degrees at the base of the petal, towards the reverse side of the petal. Lay it reverse side down in a 4½in (11.5cm) half sphere former to dry, feeding the wire down through the center hole. Smooth the petal to conform with the former. Make sure to dust the former lightly with cornstarch (cornflour) to prevent the paste from sticking. If the tip of the petal rises higher than the edge of the former, tuck a small piece of tissue behind it to prevent creases or any fold over. Make six large petals per flower.

15. As an option to make more open and side-curled petals, create the petals in the same way, but dry them in a foil former that has been shaped around a rolling pin.

ASSEMBLE THE MAGNOLIA

16. Using green half-width floral tape (see Getting Started), wrap the tape under the base of the flower center two or three times. Tape three small petals around the center one at a time, spacing them evenly.

17. Tape the first three large petals so that they lay over the openings in between the first layer of inner petals.

18. Tape the last three large petals so that they lay over the openings between the previous layer of outer petals. Tape all the way down the wires to create a single neat stem.

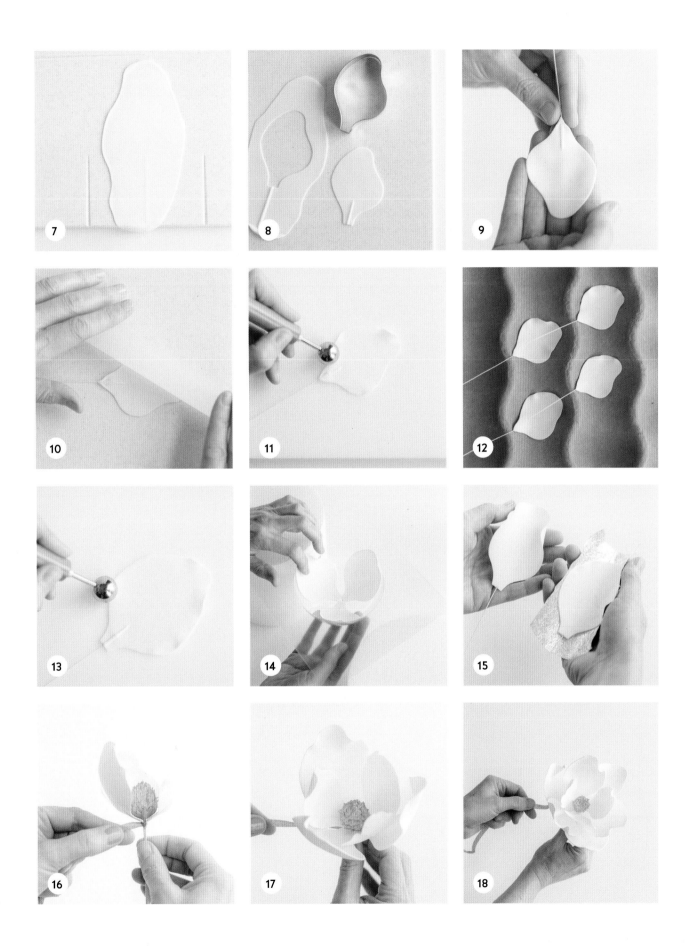

Peonies

Peonies are a wonderful flower to have in your repertoire! The techniques I share here are a great place to start, but I encourage you to play with petal sizes and finishes to create versions to fit your own design aesthetic. The open peonies have ruffled or smooth petals that are individually wired so you can gently move them as needed when arranging peonies with other flowers. The closed peony is a favorite, and my interpretation of the flower is a gorgeous ball of petals before it begins to bloom.

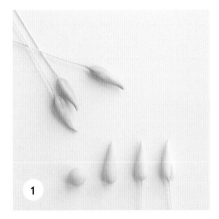

1

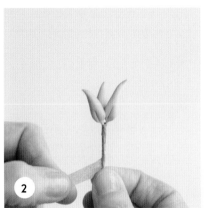

2

3

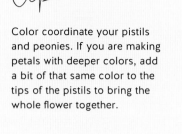

tip

Color coordinate your pistils and peonies. If you are making petals with deeper colors, add a bit of that same color to the tips of the pistils to bring the whole flower together.

4

OPEN PEONIES

SPECIFICS YOU WILL NEED

· Rose petal cutters in four sizes: 1½ x 1⅞in (4 x 4.7cm), 1⅞ x 2⅛in (4.7 x 5.3cm), 2 x 2⅜in (5 x 6cm), and 2¼ x 2⅝in (5.5 x 6.7cm)
· XL petal veiner for the ruffled peony (Sugar Art Studio)
· 2½in (6.5cm) half sphere formers with ¼in (5mm) hole in the center
· Rose petal veiner for the charm peony (SK Great Impressions)
· 2in (5cm) and 2⅜in (6cm) styrofoam balls (5–6 of each)
· Yellow stamens (medium lily tip or hammerhead tip)
· 28g and 30g white wire
· Waxed dental floss
· Floral tape (green)
· Kiwi green, cosmos pink, daffodil yellow, peach and cream petal dust
· Green (Americolor Avocado), pale pink (Wilton Pink) and pale peach (Wilton Creamy Peach) pastes

MAKE THE CENTER

1. To make the pistils, roll a small ⅜in (8mm) ball of green paste into a ⅞in (2.3cm) cone shape. Attach to a hooked 28g white wire, securing it neatly at the base (see Getting Started). Use a knife tool to make three indentations evenly spaced around the base, running a third of the way up the cone. Curl the tip gently with your fingertips. Allow it to dry. Make three pistils per peony. Dust with soft green dust all over the pistil, and add a touch of pink on the tips. Steam to set the color (see Getting Started) and let them dry before using.

2. Using half-width floral tape (see Getting Started), attach the three pistils together starting under their

bases and taping all the way down the wires to create a single stem.

3. Take a small group of around 25 yellow stamens and attach them to the pistil stem using waxed dental floss, wrapping tightly three times around to secure. Wrap the floss just under the base of the pistils to prevent any gaps between the pistils and stamens. The tops of the stamens should be a bit taller than the pistils.

4. Attach three or four more groups of stamens, evenly spaced, around the stem or until the desired fullness is achieved. Make sure to wrap tightly three times with the dental floss for each group before adding the next. Continue to step 5.

5. Once all the stamens are added, wrap the stem tightly with half-width floral tape from the base of the pistils halfway down the stamens.

6. Trim the stamen ends into a tapered point with sharp scissors to reduce bulk, and then wrap the rest of the way down with tape to create a single neat stem.

7. Gently open and spread out the stamens around the pistils to distribute them evenly. If desired, dust the stamen tips with yellow petal dust to deepen the color. Steam the peony center for a few seconds (see Getting Started) and allow it to dry before adding ruffled or charm peony petals to complete your flower.

MAKE THE RUFFLED PEONY PETALS

8. Use three graduated sizes of rose petal cutters to make the peony petals, referring to them as small, medium and large. The sizes used here are 1½ x 1⅞in (4 x 4.7cm), 1⅞ x 2⅛in (4.7 x 5.3cm), and 2 x 2⅜in (5 x 6cm). Roll pale pink paste thinly on a groove board, cut a small petal, and thin the edges with a ball tool on a foam pad. Dip a 30g wire in sugar glue and insert about ½in (1cm) into the groove. Secure at the base.

9. Using scissors, cut one small rounded v-shape out of the top of the petal.

10. Press the wired petal in a veiner.

11. Using a small ball tool on a foam pad, lightly ruffle the top edge of the petal, making sure to leave the sides and base of the petal smooth and flat as shown.

12. Using the ball tool, make three or four small strokes to cup along the top edge of the petal.

13. Gently bend the wire 90 degrees right at the base of the petal, towards the reverse side of the petal. Lay reverse side down in a 2½in (6.5cm) half sphere former, feeding the wire down through the center hole. Smooth the petal with your fingers to conform it to the cupped shape of the former. Encourage a few of the top edges to curl inward a bit with your fingers, and then allow the petal to dry completely.

14. Make five small petals, nine medium petals, and five large petals per flower. Support the backs of the larger petals with modeling tools or other small objects if needed to prevent them curling over backwards.

ASSEMBLE THE RUFFLED PEONY

15. Lay out the 19 dry peony petals in front of you in the following order: four medium, five large, five medium and five small. Using half-width floral tape, attach the first medium petal to the stem so the base of the petal is lined up with the base of the pistils.

16. Tape three more medium petals evenly spaced around the stamens to create the first layer of petals.

17. Next, tape the five large petals to the flower, one at a time, and with the petal bases laying flush below the first layer. Space the petals evenly around the flower.

18. Tape five more medium petals, evenly spaced, around the flower, lining them up to overlap between the large petals.

19. Finally, tape the five small petals, evenly spaced, around the flower, lining them up to overlap between the medium petals. Once all the petals are added, wrap the tape all the way down the wires to create a single stem.

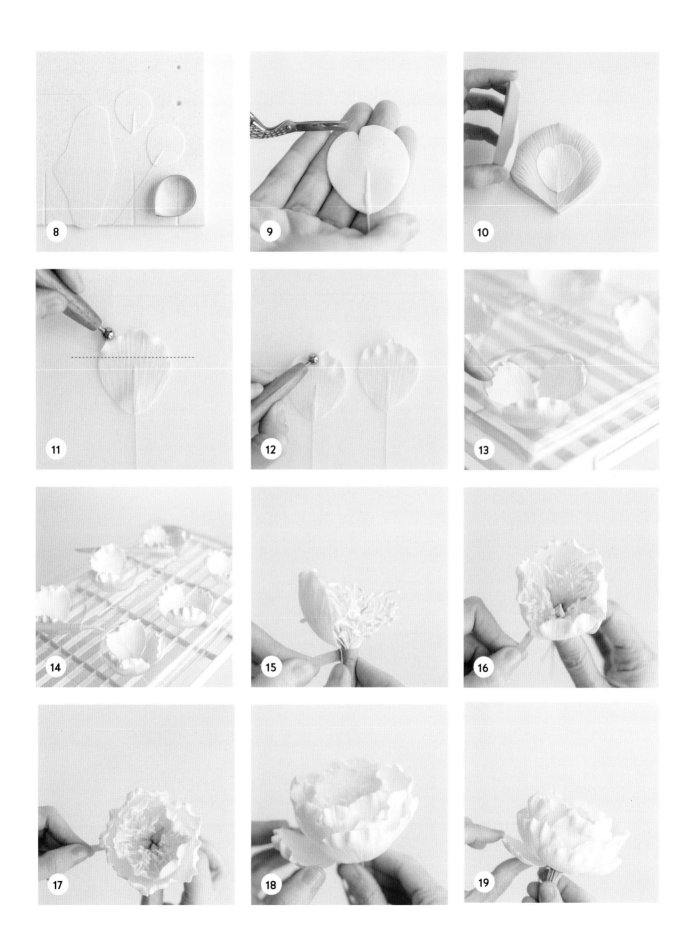

DUST THE RUFFLED PEONY

20. With a flat brush, gently dust the top edges of the peony petals with pink dust.

21. With a soft round brush, add a bit of color randomly at the base and exposed sides of the petals. Gently open the petals and steam for a few seconds to set the color. Let the petals dry before using.

MAKE THE CHARM PEONY PETALS

22. Use four graduated sizes of rose petal cutters to make the peony petals, referring to them as small, medium, large and extra large. The sizes used here are 1½ x 1⅞in (4 x 4.7cm), 1⅞ x 2⅛in (4.7 x 5.3cm), 2 x 2⅜in (5 x 6cm), and 2¼ x 2⅝in (5.5 x 6.7cm). Roll pale peach paste thinly on a groove board and cut a small petal. Thin the edges with a ball tool on a foam pad. Dip a 30g wire in sugar glue and insert into the groove (see Getting Started). Secure the wire at the base and press the wired petal in a veiner.

23. Working on the reverse side of the petal, use scissors to make a small ½in (1cm) cut into the base of the petal, close to and parallel with the wire, creating a small tab.

24. Lay the petal over a 2in (5cm) styrofoam ball, and begin smoothing it with your hand to conform it to the ball. Fold the tab of paste tightly over the wire to help the base of the petal fit snugly to the ball as well. Continue to smooth with your fingertips until the entire petal is flush with the ball. Set aside to dry.

25. Prepare between five and seven petals in all four sizes, using 2in (5cm) and 2⅜in (6cm) styrofoam balls as formers. Smaller petals on larger balls will result in less cupped petals. Larger petals on smaller styrofoam balls will result in petals that are more cupped. You want a variety of both to give the charm peony fullness and shape.

ASSEMBLE THE CHARM PEONY

26. Prepare the peony center, following steps 1–7. As with the ruffled version of the peony, use half-width floral tape to attach five or six medium petals around the stamens so that the base of the petals are lined up with the base of the pistils.

27. Next, tape a mixture of six or seven large and extra large petals to the flower, one at a time, and with the petal bases laying flush below the first layer. Space the petals evenly around the flower, layering some of them almost behind each other to create some fullness.

28. Tape five or six more medium petals, spacing them evenly, around the flower.

29. Tape a few small petals around the base of the flower to give it a beautiful shape.

30. With a flat brush, gently dust the top edges of the peony petals with a mix of peach and cream petal dust. With a soft round brush, add a bit of color randomly at the base and exposed sides of the petals. Gently open the petals and steam for a few seconds to set the color. Allow to dry completely before using.

20

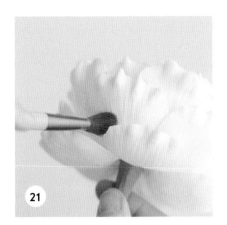

21

tip

For the charm peony petal formers, cut a small portion off the bottom of the sytrofoam balls with a craft knife so they will sit flat on a table.

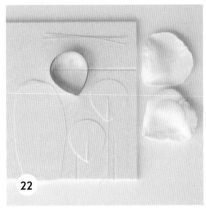

22

23

24

25

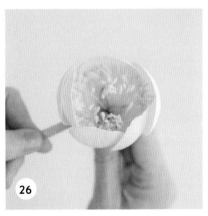

26

27

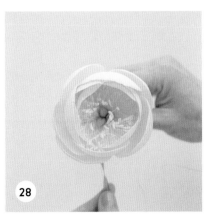

28

29

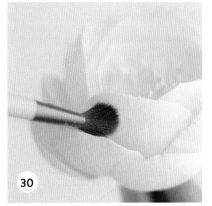

30

PEONY BUDS

SPECIFICS YOU WILL NEED

- 1½in (4cm) styrofoam ball
- 20g green wire
- Rose petal cutters in two sizes:
  1⅞ x 2⅛in (4.7 x 5.3cm) and 1⅛ x 1⅞in
  (3 x 4.7cm)
- JEM veining tool
- Cosmos pink petal dust
- Moss green petal dust
- Pale pink paste (Wilton Pink)
- Green paste (Wilton Moss Green
  and Americolor Lemon Yellow)

MAKE THE BUD

31. Glue a 1½in (4cm) styrofoam ball to a 20g wire and allow to dry.

32. Roll pale pink paste thinly and cut two 1⅞ x 2⅛in (4.7 x 5.3cm) petals. Thin the edges with a ball tool on a foam pad, then lengthen the center of the petals with a few strokes. Lightly vein the petals with the JEM veining tool.

33. Brush sugar glue on the entire surface of the petals and attach to the styrofoam ball opposite each other, overlapping one over the top of the other to hide the top of the ball. Smooth the petals to conform to the ball.

34. Make three more petals in the same way and attach them, evenly spaced, around the ball and overlapping each other, but allowing the tip of the first layer of petals to be seen.

35. Roll green paste thinly and cut three 1⅛ x 1⅞in (3 x 4.7cm) petals for the calyx and lightly vein them with the JEM veining tool.

36. Apply sugar glue to all of the petals and attach around the base of the bud evenly, with the points meeting at the wire, and hiding any bits of styrofoam that may be showing. Smooth the calyx with your fingertips to conform to the shape of the ball. Allow to dry completely.

37. Dust the petals in the same color to coordinate with your peony flowers. Add a bit of a darker shade where the petals all come together at the top of the bud.

38. Dust the calyx with moss green and then a bit of cosmos pink just on the edges. Steam for a few seconds to set the colors (see Getting Started) and let the bud dry before using.

CLOSED PEONIES

SPECIFICS YOU WILL NEED

- 2in (5cm) styrofoam ball
- 18g green wire
- 1½in (4cm) circle cutter
- Scalloped peony petal cutter, 1½ x
  1¾in (4 x 4.5cm) (Cakes by Design)
- JEM veining tool
- 2in (5cm) cupped former for
  outer petals
- Rose petal cutters in two sizes: 1⅞
  x 2⅛in (4.7 x 5.3cm), 1⅛ x 1⅞in (3 x 4.7cm)
- Cosmos pink petal dust
- Moss green petal dust
- Pale pink paste (Wilton Pink)
- Green paste (Wilton Moss Green
  and Americolor Lemon Yellow)

MAKE THE CLOSED PEONY

1. Glue a 2in (5cm) styrofoam ball to an 18g wire and allow to dry. Mark the ball with a 1½in (4cm) circle cutter and cut off the top piece with a sharp knife.

2. Using a craft knife cut around the edge of the circle and across the center with an "x", as shown, cutting about ¾in (2cm) deep. Use a small spoon to scoop out the four sections of styrofoam to create a hole in the top of the styrofoam ball.

3. Roll pale pink paste very thinly and cut 11 scalloped peony petals, 1½ x 1¾in (4 x 4.5cm) in size. Keep them covered to prevent drying.

4. Working with four petals, vein them on a firm surface with the JEM veining tool, and then cup along the top edges with a ball tool on a foam pad. Continue to step 5.

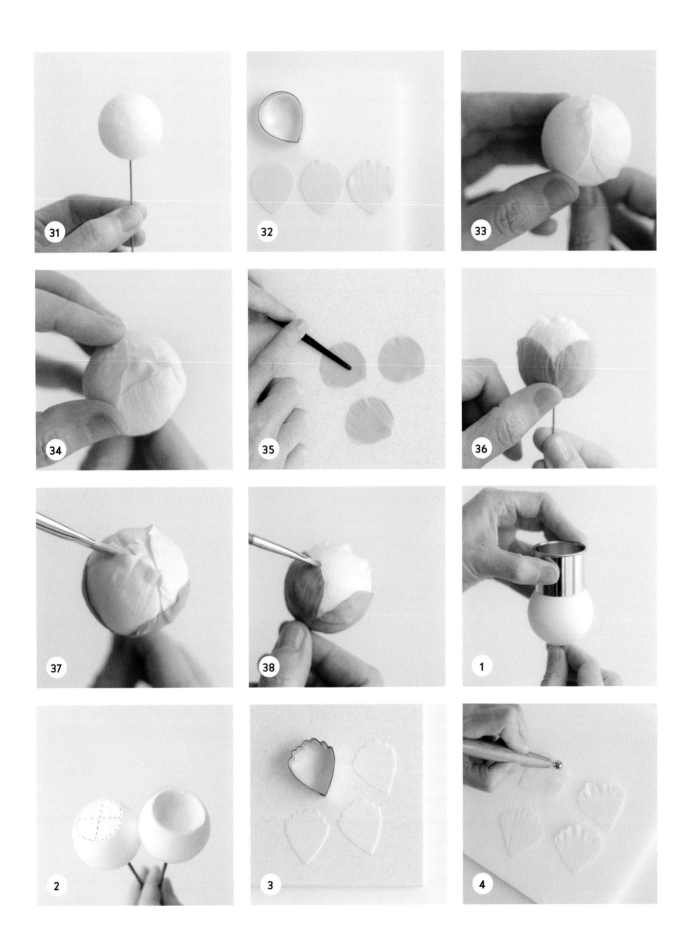

5. Apply sugar glue to the backs of the four petals, and then lay them in the hole in the styrofoam ball, overlapping the petals and allowing the cupped top edges to sit above the top edge of the hole. Use a smooth tool to help press the petals into place if necessary.

6. Repeat the same process with four more petals, and layer them over the top of the previous petals and at the same height, filling more of the hole. Don't make the petals too perfect and compact, some messiness makes it look more natural.

7. Start the last three petals in the same way, including veining and cupping the top edge. This time, dab a bit of glue in the center of the petals, and roll and scrunch them across the middle, leaving the delicate cupped top edges intact. Trim off the bottom third of the petal.

8. Apply a small amount of sugar glue to the base of the petals and use them to fill the remaining hole completely. Use the end of a rounded tool to help press and secure them in place, avoiding flattening any of the top edges. Make any additional petals as needed if there are any gaps. The center should look full and busy, but also delicate.

9. Roll pale pink paste thinly, cut five more of the same petals, and prepare them in the same way including veining and cupping the top edge.

10. Apply glue to the front of the petals avoiding the cupped top edges. Attach the petals, evenly spaced, around the styrofoam ball, using the cupped edges to hide the top rim of the opening. Smooth the petals to conform to the shape of the ball.

11. For the outer petals, roll pale pink paste thinly and cut five 1⅞ x 2⅛in (4.7 x 5.3cm) rose petals. On a firm surface, vein the petals with the JEM veining tool.

12. Cut a ¾in (2cm) slit into the base of the petals and lay them each in a 2in (5cm) cupped former, folding the tails of paste over each other to help conform to the cupped shape. Smooth the petals with your fingers, and let them dry briefly, just until they hold their shape.

13. Apply glue to the left and right edges of the insides of the petals and attach them evenly around the ball, so the tops are the same height or just barely below the center petals.

14. Repeat the same process to create five or six more of the same size petals. Apply sugar glue to the left and right edges of the inside of the petals and attach them in a second layer around the flower, offsetting the first layer of petals, but keeping them closed around the ball. Additional petals may be added as desired, attaching them lower or making them more open.

15. If desired, create and attach a calyx in the same way as steps 35–38 for the peony bud, using a 1⅛ x 1⅞in (3 x 4.7cm) rose petal cutter. If you don't wish to add a calyx but a bit of the styrofoam is showing, cut a small circle shape in the same color paste as the petals, and attach with a small amount of sugar glue. Allow to dry.

16. When made in a pretty pale pink, the closed peonies don't need much color added to them at all. Dust the top edges of the center petals with pale pink dust to highlight them. Dust the calyx with moss green dust and add some pink to the edges. Steam the peony for a few seconds to set the color, and let dry before using.

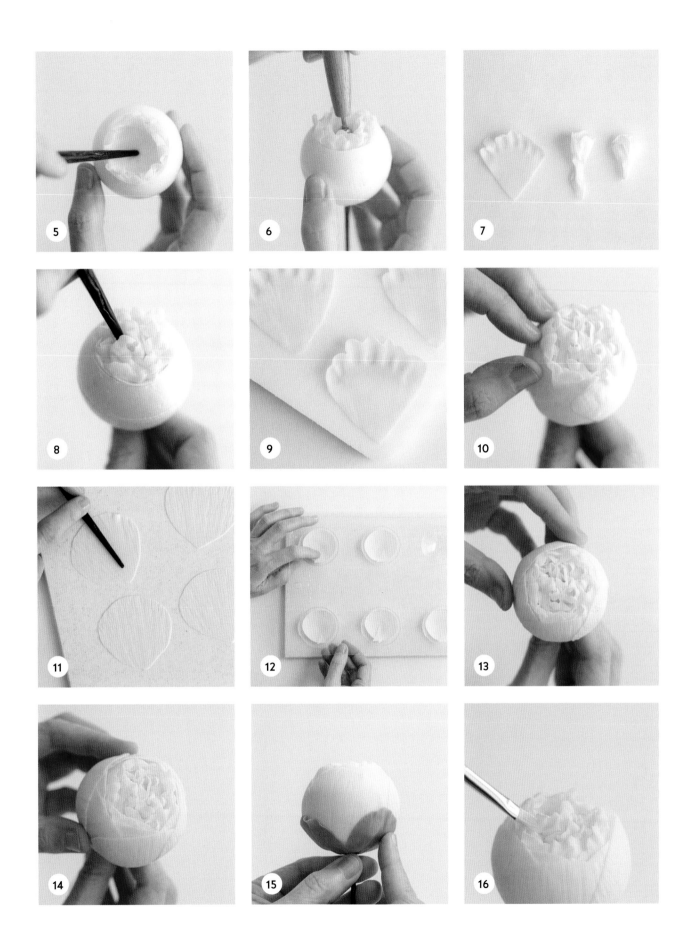

Phalaenopsis Orchid

One of the most popular orchids, the Phalaenopsis comes in a wide variety of colors including pinks and purples, and my favorite, white petals with a pop of color in the center. Even with each flower having seven pieces, they are a lot easier than they look! Take each piece one at a time, and they will all come together beautifully in the end. Phalaenopsis orchids are perfect trailing down the side of a cake, or add one layered over hydrangea and filler flowers for a clean, modern touch.

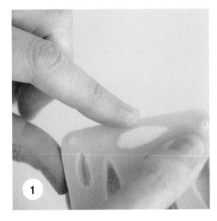

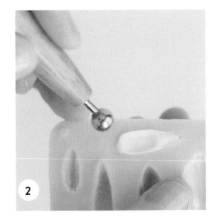

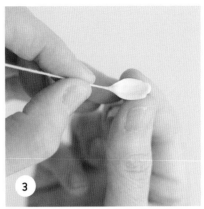

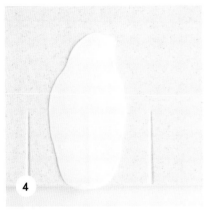

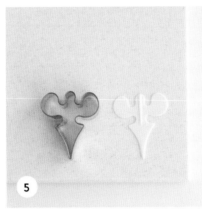

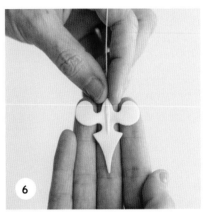

SPECIFICS YOU WILL NEED

···

- Orchid column mold (Cakes by Design)
- Orchid center cutter (SK Great Impressions or Sugar Art Studio)
- Orchid petal cutter and veiner (SK Great Impressions or Sugar Art Studio)
- Orchid sepal cutter and veiner (SK Great Impressions or Sugar Art Studio)
- Wooden skewer
- Egg crate foam
- Floral tape (white)
- Red gel color and fine paintbrush
- 30g white wire
- 22g green wire
- Daffodil yellow, magenta and kiwi green petal dust
- White paste
- Pale yellow paste (Americolor Lemon Yellow)
- Pale green paste (Americolor Avocado)

MAKE THE CENTER

1. Press a small ball of white paste into the orchid column mold. Under fill the mold a little bit to allow for some manipulation of the paste in the next step.

2. Using a small ball tool, press on the paste to hollow out the front two thirds of the column.

3. Insert a 30g hooked white wire into the back third of the column and secure it neatly at the base (see Getting Started). Allow it to dry completely.

4. Roll white paste moderately thinly, about 1/16in (2mm) on a groove board.

5. Turn the paste over so you can see the groove, and cut the orchid center shape, using the small amount of groove shown.

6. Insert a 30g white wire into the groove and secure neatly at the base. Continue to step 7.

7. Gently press the orchid center in the petal veiner to add a bit of light texture, avoiding the pointed tip.

8. Lay the center on a foam pad with the groove down. Using a ball tool, cup the outer left and right pieces of the orchid center.

9. Cut into the pointed tip with scissors, down the middle and just short of the widest part.

10. Curl both tips towards the center with a wooden skewer (or toothpick or needle tool).

11. Place the orchid center in foam to dry in a cupped shape. Let it dry completely.

12. Roll two tiny balls of yellow paste for the callus. Glue them together and then attach them to the orchid center. Let them dry completely before dusting.

MAKE THE PETALS

13. Roll white paste moderately thinly on a groove board and cut the petal shape with minimal groove as shown. This will prevent a shadow of the wire showing through the petals.

14. Insert a 30g white wire into the groove and secure neatly at the base. Thin the edge of the petal with a ball tool on a foam pad.

15. Press the wired petal in the petal veiner.

16. The petals can be dried flat, gently cupped, or with some bits of tissue or foam under them to give the impression of movement. Make two petals per orchid.

MAKE THE SEPALS

17. Roll white paste moderately thinly on a groove board, and cut a sepal shape with minimal groove as shown.

18. Insert a 30g white wire and secure neatly at the base. Thin the edge of the sepal with a ball tool on a foam pad. Continue to step 19.

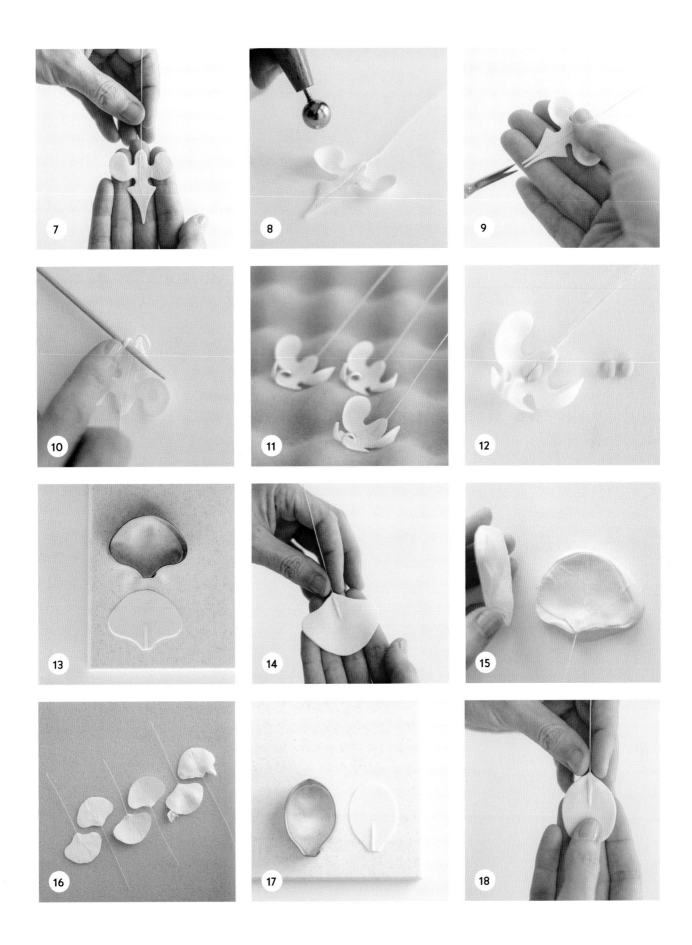

19. Press the wired sepal in the orchid sepal veiner.

20. It is important to dry the sepals consistently with the shape of the petals, otherwise they will not fit together when you go to tape them. If you dried your two petals flat or with some movement, dry the sepals flat as well, or lay them front-side down in a lightly cupped flower former so they will curve gently away from the petals. If you dried your petals so they are cupped towards you, then dry the sepals exactly the same way. Make three sepals per flower.

DUST AND ASSEMBLE THE ORCHID

21. Dust the middle of the orchid center with yellow dust, covering over the callus and dusting on both sides of it.

22. Dust all of the edges and tips with dark pink or magenta dust.

23. Using a tiny brush or end of a toothpick, add little dots with red gel color to the callus and across the center of the orchid.

24. Dust the front of the column with pink. Dust the back and a bit of the underside of the column with yellow dust. Add small dots with red gel color in the cupped underside of the column. Let the dots dry.

25. Using half-width white floral tape, attach the column and center together tightly. Gently steam for a few seconds to set the color (see Getting Started). Allow to dry before adding the petals and sepals.

26. Tape on the two petals to the left and right of the center.

27. Tape on the three sepals, one at a time, so they are flush behind the two petals and creating a triangle shape. Attach one sepal at the top so it can be seen between the two petals, and then the other two sepals so they just peek out below the other petals, one to the left and one to the right. Tape all the way down the wires to create a single stem.

MAKE THE BUDS

28. Roll a small ball of pale green paste until smooth, and secure it neatly to a hooked 22g green wire.

29. Using the knife tool, make three indentations evenly spaced around the ball, running from the top to the bottom of the bud. Let it dry completely.

30. Dust the indentations of the bud with kiwi green dust, and add a bit of pink (or another matching color from the flowers) to the tip of the bud. Steam for a few seconds to set the color and allow to dry before using.

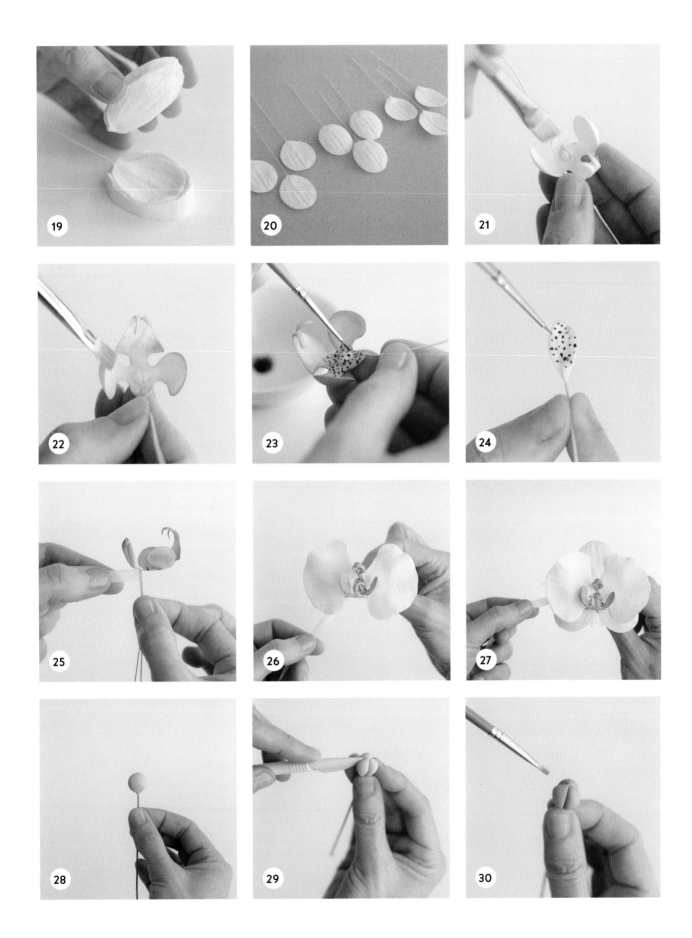

Ranunculus

An adorable springtime favorite, the ranunculus is made up
of layers of delicate petals with a pop of green in the center.
Our standard size flower is created with five or six layers. The
key is to practice making and attaching the petals so you can
easily build on our basic flower when you have time to play and
create. Make a single over-bloomed ranunculus as a statement
flower on a mini-cake, or keep them more uniform and tuck
them into a topper.

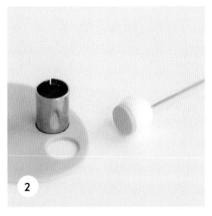

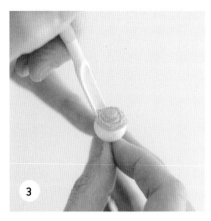

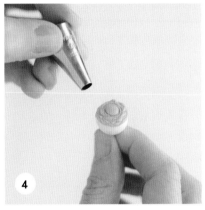

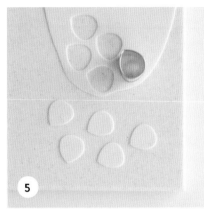

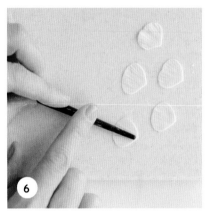

SPECIFICS YOU WILL NEED

···

- ⅝in (1.5cm) styrofoam ball
- 20g green wire
- ½in (1cm) circle cutter
- No.10 round piping tip (nozzle)
- Scallop modeling tool
- Metal rose petal cutters (press gently to flatten across the top edge) in four sizes: ½ x ⅝in (1 x 1.5cm), ¾ x ⅞in (2 x 2.3cm), 1 x 1in (2.5 x 2.5cm) and 1¼ x 1¼in (3.2 x 3.2cm) (Cakes by Design)
- JEM veining tool
- 1⅞in (4.7cm) calyx cutter (Cakes by Design or Sunflower Sugar Art)
- Cosmos pink petal dust
- Kiwi green petal dust
- Moss green petal dust
- Pale green paste (Americolor Avocado)
- Pale pink paste (Wilton Pink)

MAKE THE CENTER

1. Glue a ⅝in (1.5cm) styrofoam ball to a green 20g wire and cut off approximately the top third with a craft knife, creating a ½in (1cm) flat surface.

2. Roll green paste to ⅛in (3mm) thickness and cut a ½in (1cm) circle shape. Apply sugar glue to the circle, and attach it to the flat surface on the styrofoam ball.

3. Press randomly around the circle and out around the edge of the paste with a scallop modeling tool, letting the impressions overlap, creating the look of layers of petals.

4. Press firmly into the center of the paste with the end of a No.10 round piping tip (nozzle) to make a raised circle. Let the center dry for a few hours before adding the petals.

MAKE THE PETALS

5. Roll pale pink paste to 1⁄16in (2mm) thickness and cut five of the smallest sized petals, measuring ½ x ⅝in (1 x 1.5cm).

6. On a firm surface, vein the petals with the JEM veining tool. Continue to step 7.

7. Using the ball tool on a foam pad, cup each petal completely starting in the center and circling all the way out to the petal edges.

8. Turn the petals upside down for a few seconds until they hold their shape.

9. Apply a small amount of sugar glue in a v-shape along the inner left and right edges of the petals. Attach the five petals about ¼in (5mm) higher over the center, evenly spaced, and tucking the edge of the last petal under the first.

10. Repeat with the second layer of five of the same size petals, placing the first petal at the same height and so that it overlaps where two petals meet in the first layer. Evenly space the remaining petals, tucking the edge of the last petal under the first.

11. Make five petals with the ¾ x ⅞in (2 x 2.3cm) size cutter to create the third layer. When attaching these petals, make them the same height, but a tiny bit more open, creating space between the layers. This flower at this stage can be used as a bud.

12. Repeat with a second round of the same size petals, using six petals for the fourth layer, and attaching them so they are a bit more open.

13. Make six petals with the 1 x 1in (2.5 x 2.5cm) size cutter to create the fifth layer. A sixth layer can be added using six or seven larger petals using the 1¼ x 1¼in (3.2 x 3.2cm) size cutter. Each layer should be a little bit more open.

14. To make a flower that is very bloomed, make a few more petals in the same size you used last for a more compact flower, or the next size larger for a more dramatically open flower. Attach them randomly, placing them lower on the flower and open, or at the same height but very open (see photographs 17 and 18). Let the ranunculus dry completely before dusting.

MAKE THE CALYX (OPTIONAL)

15. Roll green paste thinly and cut a 1⅞in (4.7cm) calyx shape. Cup the widest part of the calyx with a ball tool on a foam pad. Apply sugar glue to the center and tips of the calyx.

16. Attach the calyx to the base of the ranunculus flower or bud and smooth with your fingers. Allow it to dry completely.

DUST THE RANUNCULUS

17. Dust the ranunculus centers with kiwi green. Dust outwards from the center over the first or second layer of petals. Dust the calyx with moss green and spread a little of the green onto the base of the flower.

18. Dust the top edges of the petals with cosmos pink. Steam to set the colors (see Getting Started) and allow to dry before using.

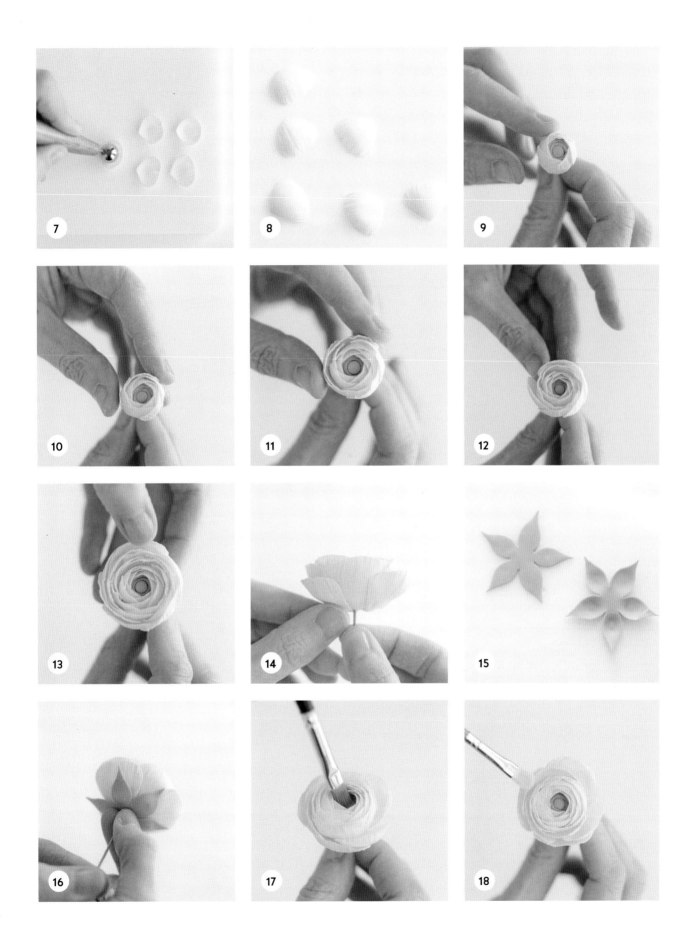

English Rose

This English-style rose is a beautiful combination of a delicate round center, surrounded by two layers of petals that are open and relaxed. You can easily add a few additional layers of outer petals to create a heavily bloomed flower. The classic soft peach tones are a perfect mix with green hydrangea and rose leaves, but these roses are also stunning in shades of pink.

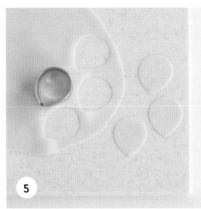

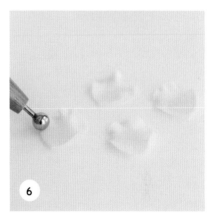

SPECIFICS YOU WILL NEED

·····················

- 1½in (4cm) styrofoam ball
- 20g green wire
- ⅞in (2.3cm) circle cutter
- Craft knife
- Rose petal cutters in five sizes:
  ¾ x ⅞in (2 x 2.3cm), 1⅜ x 1⅝in (3.5 x
  4.3cm), 1½ x 1⅞in (4 x 4.7cm), 1⅞ x 2⅛in
  (4.7 x 5.3cm) and 2 x 2⅜in (5 x 6cm)
- XL rose petal veiner (Marcel
  Veldbloem Flower Veiners)
- Small scissors
- 3in (7.5cm) calyx cutter (JEM Large
  Rose Calyx)
- 2in (5cm) half sphere cupped formers
- 2½in (6.5cm) half sphere cupped
  formers
- Peach petal dust
- Moss green petal dust
- White paste
- Pale peach paste (Wilton Creamy
  Peach)
- Green paste (Americolor Avocado
  and Lemon Yellow)

MAKE THE CENTER

1. Glue a 1½in (4cm) styrofoam ball to
a 20g wire.

2. Mark a circle on the top of the ball
with a ⅞in (2.3cm) circle cutter and
cut off that portion with a sharp knife.

3. Use a craft knife to cut an "x"
shape across the flat top, about ½in
(1cm) deep and then cut around the
edge of the circle at the same depth.

4. Use a small spoon to lift out the
quarter pieces of styrofoam and
press down on any rough spots with

your fingers. The hole created in the
ball does not have to be perfectly
smooth, just clean enough to fill with
petals.

5. Roll pale peach paste very thinly
to ½₂in (1mm) and cut eight ¾ x ⅞in
(2 x 2.3cm) rose petals.

6. Thin the petals on a foam pad
with a ball tool and lightly ruffle the
top edges to give them movement.
Continue to step 7.

7. Apply sugar glue to the reverse side of the petals, and place four petals evenly spaced around the inside edge of the hole in the styrofoam center.

8. Prepare the remaining four petals in the same way, and then roll them up into open cones and pinch them at the base.

9. Apply sugar glue to the base of the rolled petals and place them randomly into the opening to fill the center of the rose. Use the round end of a brush or small Celpin to secure them in place. Make a few more petals if you need them to fill in any gaps. Don't fill the center with too many petals or it will look heavy. Allow space between the petals so the center looks light and airy.

MAKE THE INNER PETALS

10. Cut five ¾ x ⅞in (2 x 2.3cm) petals and thin the edges with a ball tool. Apply sugar glue to the entire surface of the petals and place them, evenly spaced, around the center so they cover any edge of the styrofoam opening that may be visible.

11. Cut five 1⅜ x 1⅝in (3.5 x 4.3cm) petals and thin the edges with a ball tool. As you did with the smaller petals, apply glue to the whole surface of the petals and evenly space them around the center, laying them flat on the ball. Pinch the petals at the base to help them conform to the round ball shape. Trim off the excess paste with scissors and smooth any seams with your fingers.

12. Repeat the same process with another five petals of the same size, overlapping the joins of the petals in the previous layer.

13. Lighten the paste color you are using by at least 50 per cent by mixing in some white paste. This will help give the rose center some depth and dimension, and will make the outer petals look more delicate. Roll the paste thinly and cut five 1½ x 1⅞in (4 x 4.7cm) petals. Thin the edges with a ball tool and press in a rose petal veiner.

14. Cut a ½in (1cm) slit into the base of the petals with scissors.

15. Smooth the petals into a 2in (5cm) cupped former, crossing over the two tips to help the petals conform to the cupped shape. Allow to dry for 1 or 2 minutes until they hold their cupped shape.

16. Apply a small amount of glue in a v-shape along the inside left and right edges of the petals. Attach them, evenly spaced, around the rose center with the petals slightly open at the top, tucking the last petal under the first.

17. Repeat the same process with a second set of the same size petals. This time when you attach them, make them a little bit more open at the top.

18. Cut five 1⅞ x 2⅛in (4.7 x 5.3cm) petals, thin the edges and press in a rose petal veiner. Prepare them in the same way, cutting a slit in the base, crossing the tips, and laying them in the 2in (5cm) cupped former until they hold their shape. Continue to step 19.

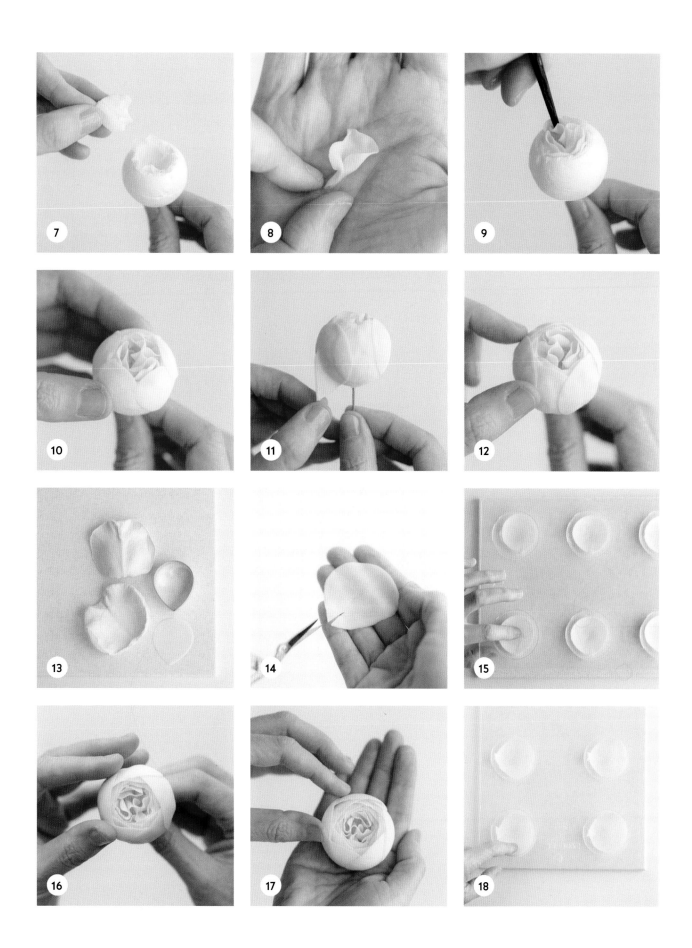

19. Apply a small amount of glue in a v-shape along the inside left and right edges of the petals. Attach the petals, evenly spaced around the flower, and a bit more open at the top. This will finish the rose center.

MAKE THE OUTER PETALS

20. Make two more of the same size petals, as in step 18.

21. Apply sugar glue in a v-shape along the inside left and right edges of the petals and attach them to the flower so they are approximately opposite one another, and more open.

22. Cut three 2 x 2⅜in (5 x 6cm) petals, thin the edges with a ball tool and press them in a rose veiner. Add a bit of ruffle to the top edges if desired. Lay them in a 2½in (6.5cm) cupped former until they are just dry enough to hold their shape.

23. Apply glue in a v-shape to the left and right edges of the petals and attach them to the flower, filling in spaces and making them a bit more open. If the petals are too long, trim them at the base with scissors. The trick here is to not make the finished flower too round or symmetrical, but instead to offset the round center. Additional open petals may be added as desired. Hang to dry, placing small bits of foam or tissue between the outer petals to keep them open and in position.

MAKE THE CALYX (OPTIONAL)

24. Roll green paste thinly and cut a 3in (7.5cm) calyx shape.

25. Thin the edges with a ball tool on a foam pad.

26. Make additional small snips into the calyx with scissors, creating delicate edges.

27. Roughen up the edges of the calyx by going over them with a small ball tool until they begin to curl and look a bit ruffled.

28. Turn the calyx over, apply sugar glue to the center and sections of the calyx, and then attach it to the base of the flower. Let the flower dry completely.

DUST THE ROSE AND CALYX

29. Dust the center petals of the rose with very pale peach dust, leaving the outer petals as they are to keep them light and delicate.

30. Dust moss green on the calyx, and spread a bit of the color around the base of the rose. Steam to set the colors (see Getting Started) and allow to dry before using.

tip

To help find the right fit and look, try holding the outer petals in different places before adding the sugar glue and attaching them to the flower.

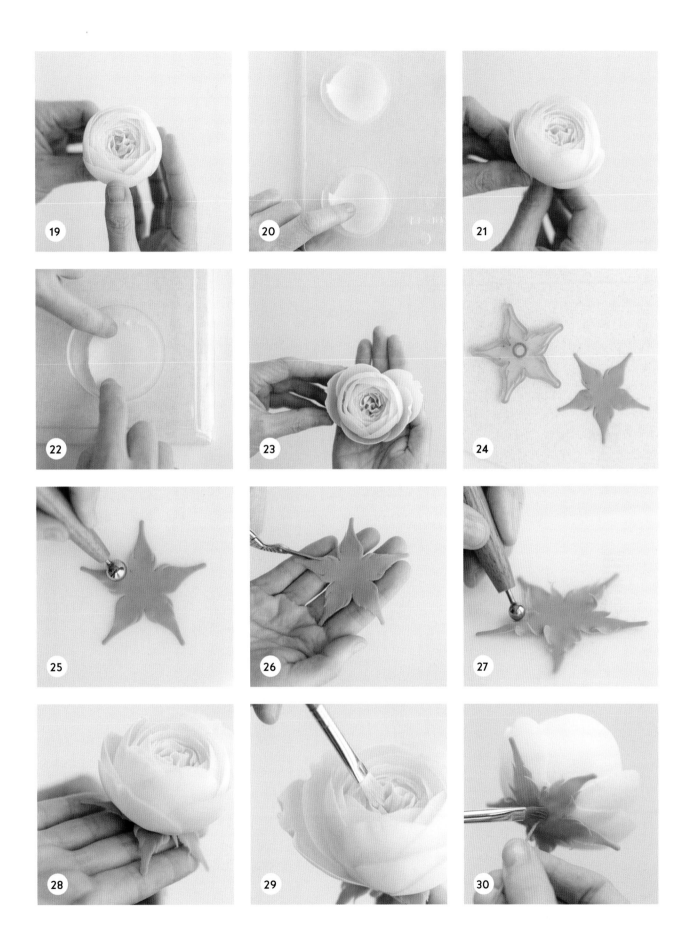

Garden Rose

This versatile garden rose is created in two phases. First, make the delicate wired petals and let them dry. Second, make the layered rose center, and while it's still soft, use three of the dry wired petals as a former to dry the center. Using this technique, the fresh rose center and dried petals will fit together seamlessly without any gaps. With all the lovely texture from the layers of petals, this is a great flower to perch on the top edge of a cake.

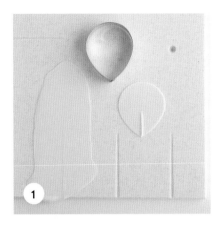
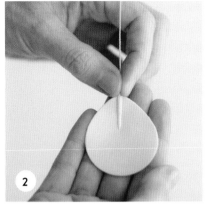

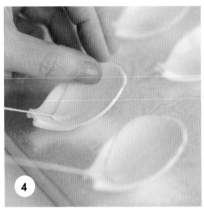
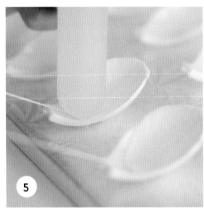
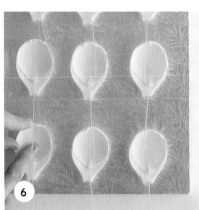

SPECIFICS YOU WILL NEED

....

- Rose petal cutters in four sizes:
  ⅞ x 1in (2.3 x 2.5cm), 1⅛ x 1⅜in
  (3 x 3.5cm), 1½ x 1⅞in (4 x 4.7cm)
  and 1⅞ x 2⅛in (4.7 x 5.3cm)
- Large rose petal veiner (SK Great
  Impressions)
- 30g white wire
- 20g green wire
- Plastic soup spoons as petal
  formers
- 2½in (6.5cm) half sphere cupped
  formers
- Small scissors
- Floral tape (green)
- Celbud2 (20mm)
- Cosmos pink petal dust
- Pale pink paste (Wilton Pink)

MAKE THE SMALL WIRED PETALS

1. Roll pale pink paste thinly on a groove board and cut a 1½ x 1⅞in (4 x 4.7cm) rose petal. Thin edges with a ball tool on a foam pad.

2. Dip a 30g white wire in sugar glue and insert into the paste. Secure by gently pinching where the wire enters the paste (see Getting Started).

3. Press the wired petal in a rose veiner.

4. Gently press and smooth the petal into a plastic soup spoon, curling tiny bits of the paste in the petal over the top edges of the spoon. Don't

curl over the entire top edge of the petal, but instead make the bits more random for a delicate look. Be sure to put a bit of cornstarch (cornflour) on the spoon to prevent the paste from sticking too unevenly around the top edges and then allowing air bubbles to form under the petals.

5. Press on the base of the petal with a ball tool or rounded rolling pin so the paste and wire conform to the cupped shape of the spoon.

6. Make 12 small petals and let them dry completely.

MAKE THE MEDIUM WIRED PETALS

7. Repeat the same process, cutting a 1⅞ x 2⅛in (4.7 x 5.3cm) petal. Thin the edges, secure a 30g white wire, and press in a rose veiner.

8. Gently press and smooth the petal into the same size soup spoon, curling tiny bits of the paste in the petal over the top edge of the spoon. Don't curl over the entire top edge of the petal, but instead make the bits more random for a delicate look. Do not fold over the sides of the petals. Press on the base of the petal with a ball tool or rounded rolling pin so that the paste and wire conform to the cupped shape of the spoon.

9. Make six medium petals and let them dry completely.

MAKE THE CUPPED WIRED PETALS

10. Repeat the same process, cutting three more of the 1⅞ x 2⅛in (4.7 x 5.3cm) petals. Thin the edges, secure a 30g white wire, and press in a rose veiner. Place each petal in a 2½in (6.5cm) cupped former, folding bits of the top edge of the petal over the top edge of the former.

11. Press on the base of the petal with a ball tool or rounded rolling pin so that the wire conforms to the cupped shape of the former. Let the three cupped petals dry completely.

MAKE THE CENTER

You will need three of the small dried wired petals to use as a guide and "former" for the finished center of the rose.

12. Glue a Celbud2 (20mm) to a 20g wire.

13. Roll pale pink paste very thinly, to about ¹⁄₃₂in (1mm), and cut three ⅞ x 1in (2.3 x 2.5cm) petals. Press the petals in a rose veiner and apply sugar glue to the entire surface of the petals. Attach them, evenly spaced, around the Celbud in a tight spiral covering the tip.

14. Cut three more petals of the same size, press them in a rose veiner, cup with a ball tool on a foam pad and lightly ruffle the top edges. Apply glue to the bottom half of the petals. Attach them, evenly spaced, around the center, positioning them slightly higher than the center and making them a bit more open.

15. Repeat with three more petals, attaching them a bit higher and making them a bit more open again.

16. Repeat with three more petals, attaching them a bit higher and making them a little more open.

17. Cut three larger 1⅛ x 1⅜in (3 x 3.5cm) petals and prepare them in the same way. Attach them a bit higher.

18. Repeat with three more petals, attaching them a bit higher and making them a bit more open. Continue to step 19.

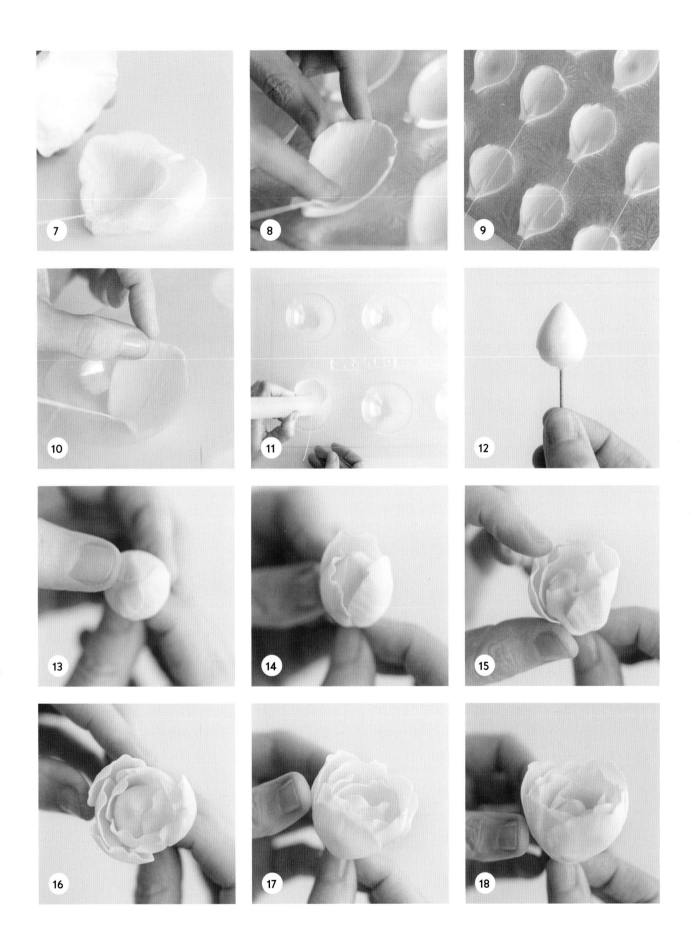

19. At this point, use one of the small dried wire petals to spot check the height and size of the rose center. The dried petal should be slightly taller than the last layer of attached petals, and should fit neatly around the base of the center.

20. If the base of the rose center is a bit wide or misshapen, trim away bits with scissors as necessary to accommodate three of the small wired petals.

21. Using half-width floral tape, attach three small dried wired petals around the rose center to help maintain its shape. The wired petals will act as a "former" so the center and the outer dried petals fit together well and look natural. Use bits of foam or tissue as needed to support or position the inner petals in the shape desired.

22. Let the rose center dry completely with the taped wired petals in place.

ASSEMBLE THE ROSE

All the wired petals will be attached in groups of three except the final layer.

23. Using half-width floral tape, attach three small petals to line up between the previous layer already in place.

24. Gather the six medium petals and attach them in the same way, in two layers of three petals each.

25. Gather the three medium cupped petals, and attach them in the same way.

26. Attach the remaining small petals, using five or six of them depending on the shape desired. Tape all the way down to cover the wires and create a single stem.

DUST THE ROSE

27. Using a dense round brush, dust cosmos pink in random circles and spots on the outside and at the base of the petals. Add a bit of color to the center of the flower as well.

28. Using a flat brush, add a bit of pink to the top of the petal edges.

29. Gently open the petals and steam the rose for a few seconds to set the color (see Getting Started). Let it dry before using.

19

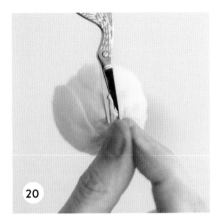

20

21

22

23

24

25

tip

For variety, make some of the garden roses with just two or three layers of outer petals, and mix them with the full garden roses. The different size roses will be more natural in an arrangement.

26

27

28

29

Climbing Rose

Small, dainty and delicate, these climbing roses are made using two five-petal rose cutter shapes. The first is wrapped around a cone in a more classic spiral, but the second is attached with no rules for the placement of the individual petals, so you don't have to worry about the flower having a perfect, symmetrical shape. In fact, the more irregular the better! They are adorable clustered together in small branches as shown, but you can also use them in small bunches or as single filler flowers too.

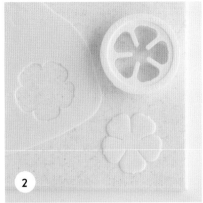

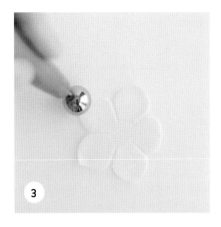

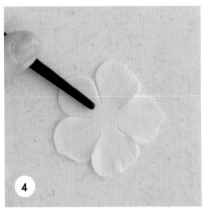

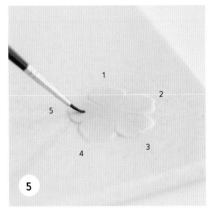

SPECIFICS YOU WILL NEED

....

- Five-petal flower cutters in three sizes: 1⅜in (3.5cm), 1½in (4cm) and 2in (5cm) (FMM 35mm and 40mm, and JEM 50mm)
- ⅞in (2.3cm) calyx cutter (PME)
- 26g green wire
- JEM veining tool
- Small scissors
- Groove board
- Needle tool
- Styrofoam dummies for drying
- Floral tape (green)
- Cosmos pink petal dust
- Kiwi green petal dust
- Pale pink paste (Wilton Pink)
- Green paste (Americolor Avocado and Lemon Yellow)

MAKE THE BUDS

1. Roll a ⅜in (8mm) ball of pale pink paste into a chunky cone shape, and secure it to a 26g hooked wire (see Getting Started). Let it dry completely.

2. Roll soft pink paste thinly to ⅙in (2mm) and cut out a single 1⅜in (3.5cm) five-petal shape.

3. On a foam pad, thin the edges with a ball tool and stretch the centers of the petals outwards to modify their shape slightly.

4. Vein the petals quickly using the JEM veining tool. If they stick to each other at the sides, gently cut them apart at the base with scissors.

5. Turn the five-petal shape over and apply sugar glue to all of the petals. Referring to the petals as 1–5 (as shown), attach to the bud center in the order given in steps 6–8.

6. Wrap petal 1 around the cone tightly, covering the tip. Continue to step 7.

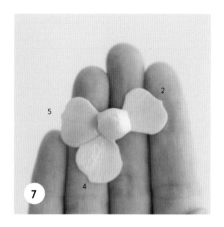

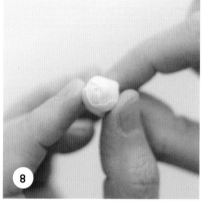

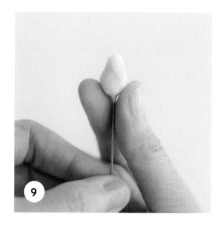

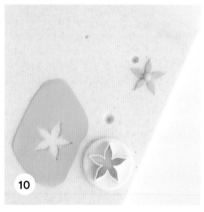

7. Next wrap petal 3 around the cone tightly.

8. Wrap the remaining petals around the cone, starting with petal 5, then 2, then 4.

9. Smooth the base of the bud with your fingers to make it rounded.

MAKE THE CALYX

10. Roll green paste over the medium (³⁄₁₆in/4mm) hole of a groove board and cut a ⁷⁄₈in (2.3cm) calyx shape.

11. Thin the calyx edges and lengthen the sections with a ball tool on a foam pad.

12. Make small snips into the calyx edges with scissors. Turn the calyx over then cup each section with a ball tool.

13. Apply a small amount of sugar glue in the middle of the calyx and on each of the sections. Attach to the base of the bud, smoothing a few sections to the bud and letting a few be more open. Allow to dry completely.

MAKE THE SMALL ROSES

14. Roll a small ⅜in (8mm) ball of pale pink paste into a narrow cone and secure to a 26g hooked wire. The size of the cone should be a bit shorter than the length of one of the 1³⁄₈in (3.5cm) flower cutter petals. Let it dry completely.

15. Roll paste thinly to ¹⁄₁₆in (2mm) and cut two 1³⁄₈in (3.5cm) flowers.

16. Thin the edges and stretch the center of the petals using a ball tool on a foam pad.

17. Vein the petals quickly with the JEM veining tool. Separate the edges with scissors if they stick together. Referring to the petals as 1–5 (as shown), attach the petals to the center cone as described in steps 18–20.

18. Apply glue to petals 1, 3 and 5. Wrap petal 1 completely around the cone in a tight spiral, covering the tip.

19. Attach petals 3 and 5 in a tight spiral.

20. Apply glue to the right sides of petals 2 and 4. Attach them in a spiral leaving the left edges open, as shown.

21. Working with the second flower shape, thin the edges and stretch the centers of the petals with a ball tool. Vein with a JEM veining tool.

22. Apply a small amount of sugar glue to the lower half of each petal, and attach them to the center randomly around the flower, letting some overlap. Continue to step 23.

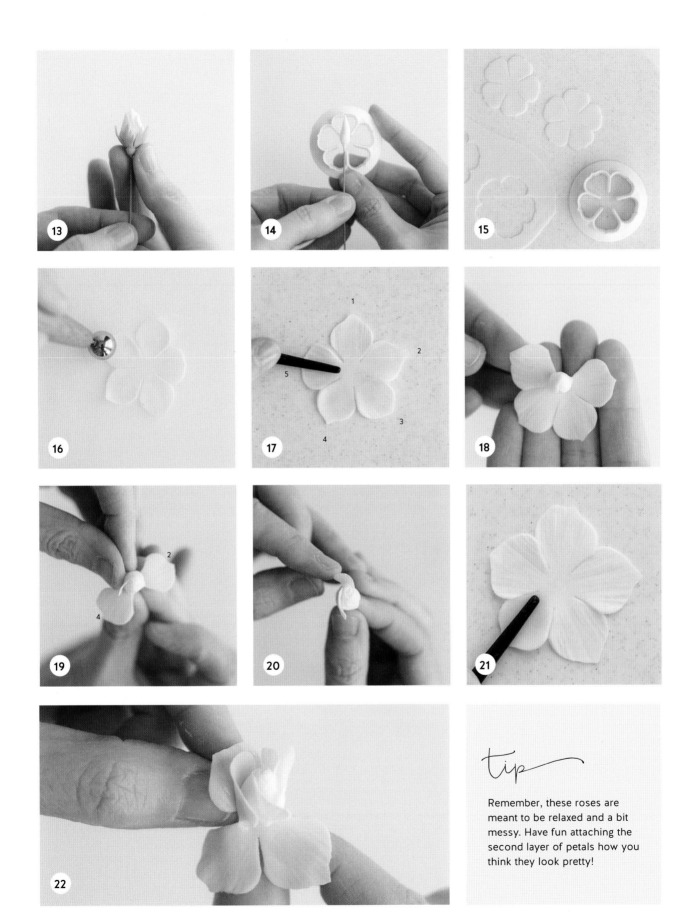

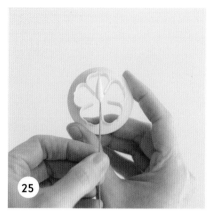

23. Allow some of the petals to be more open.

24. Make and attach a calyx in the same way as for the rose bud.

MAKE THE MEDIUM AND LARGE ROSES

25. Roll a small ⅜in (8mm) ball of pale pink paste into a narrow cone and secure to a 26g hooked wire. The size of the cone should be a bit shorter than the length of one of the 1½in (4cm) flower cutter petals. Let it dry completely.

26. Roll paste to ¹⁄₁₆in (2mm) and cut two 1½in (4cm) flowers for the medium rose or one 1½in (4cm) and one 2in (5cm) flower for the large rose. Refer to the petals as 1–5 (as shown).

27. Stretch and vein the petals of the 1½in (4cm) flower in the same way as with the small rose. Apply sugar glue to petals 1 and 3 and wrap them tightly around the cone in a spiral. Apply glue around the right side of petals 2, 4 and 5 and attach them in a loose, open spiral by smoothing down the right sides of the petals and leaving the left sides open as shown.

28. Prepare the second flower shape in the same way, but use the needle tool (or a mini Celpin or toothpick) to curl the edges of the petals forwards and back randomly. There should be a variety between all the petals.

29. Apply sugar glue to the lower half of each petal and attach to the flower in two layers. Attach petals 1 and 3 opposite each other, and then petals 2, 4 and 5 spaced randomly around the flower. Allow the flower to be a bit misshapen, avoiding a symmetrical shape. Allow one or more of the petals to be very open from the flower to add to the whimsical shape.

30. Dry the medium and large flowers with the most open petal hanging down from the flower. Sticking them into the side of a styrofoam dummy is a great way to allow the open petals to hold their shape while drying.

31. Make a calyx in the same way as for the bud and small flowers, and attach it to the base of the rose. Allow it to dry.

DUST THE ROSES AND BUDS

32. Dust cosmos pink all over the rose buds, and a medium shade of pink in the centers of the buds where the petals come together.

33. Dust cosmos pink on all of the petal edges. Add a bit of a medium shade of pink to the rose centers to highlight where the petals come together.

34. Dust kiwi green on the calyxes and a bit onto the underside of the flowers and buds. Gently steam to set the colors (see Getting Started) and let the roses dry before using.

ASSEMBLE IN A SMALL BRANCH

35. Using half-width floral tape (see Getting Started), gather several buds at varying heights and tape them together leaving long stems.

36. Wrap the tape down the wires and attach a couple of small roses, taping over the wire ¼in (5mm) from their bases. Attach a small leaf or two (see Additional Leaves), taping over the wire at their base.

37. Wrap the tape farther down the wires and attach a couple of larger roses (as shown). Continue as desired.

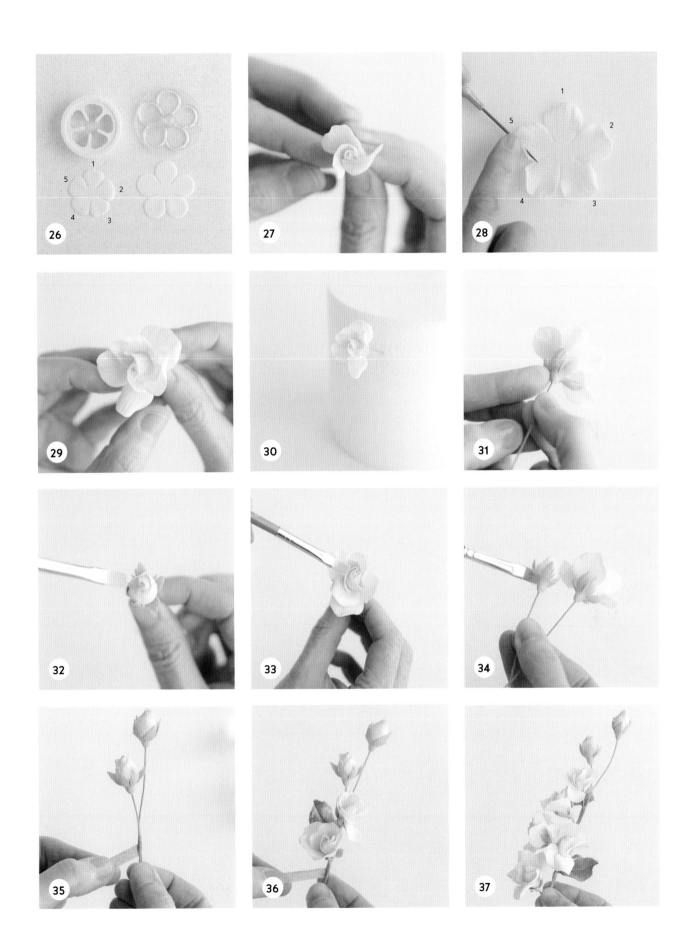

Sweet Pea

A springtime and personal favorite, sweet peas are grown in a variety of colors, mostly pastel shades of pink, purple, blue and white. Make them in four pretty stages of bloom including a bud, a partially open flower, a closed flower, and the fully bloomed sweet pea. The tiny calyxes finish them cleanly, and are worth the little bit of extra work. Sweet peas are beautiful simply gathered into a small bouquet, or tape a few flowers and buds together into a stem so they peek out between larger flowers.

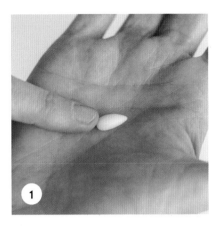

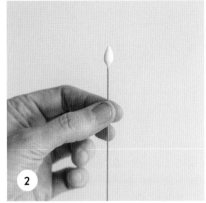

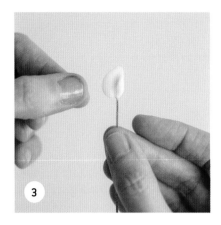

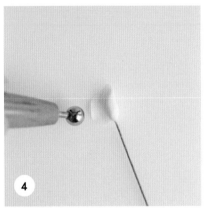

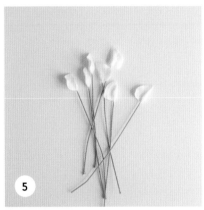

tip

If you make any centers that are just too large to use in the sweet pea flowers, save them to use as sweet pea buds. They will be perfect peeking out of an arrangement!

SPECIFICS YOU WILL NEED

- Sweet pea flower cutters (PME Medium)
- ⅝in (1.5cm) six-petal cutter for the calyx (Orchard Products)
- 26g green wire
- Single-sided petal veiner (Cakes by Design)
- Hanging rack
- Spoons
- Cosmos pink petal dust
- Kiwi green petal dust
- White paste
- Green paste (Americolor Avocado and Lemon Yellow)

MAKE THE CENTERS

1. Roll a ¼in (5mm) ball of white paste into a ½in (1cm) long cone shape.

2. Attach the cone neatly to hooked 26g wire (see Getting Started).

3. Pinch along one side and just over the tip of the cone firmly with your thumb and fingers to flatten.

4. Smooth the flattened section with a ball tool on a foam pad. Make a second pass with the ball tool on the outer edge to add a slight ruffle or wave. If needed, gently press the reverse side of the center between your fingers to keep it from getting too wide. Allow to dry completely before using.

5. Make a center for every sweet pea flower, plus a few more to use as buds.

MAKE THE INNER PETALS

6. Roll white paste thinly to ⅟₁₆in (2mm) and keep it covered to prevent drying.

7. Press individual spots on the paste firmly and evenly with a petal veiner.

8. Cut the inner petal shapes by centering the cutter over the veining.

9. Place the petals on a foam pad with the veining facing down. Thin the outer edges with a ball tool.

10. Go around the edges again with more ball tool pressure to lightly ruffle them.

11. Apply a small amount of sugar glue to the reverse side of the sweet pea center.

12. Attach the inner petal with the veining facing towards you and the notch lining up over the base of the center. Smooth the petal to the center to secure.

13. Hang the sweet pea to dry to help keep the petals from opening too wide. Let it dry completely before adding the outer petals. These can also be used as partially open versions of sweet peas.

MAKE THE OUTER PETALS

14. Prepare the paste in the same way as for the inner petals, including veining, and then cut the outer petals.

15. Place the petals with the veining side down on the foam pad, and thin the edges with a ball tool. Then lightly ruffle the edges of the petals.

16. Apply a small amount of sugar glue down the middle of the reverse side of the inner petal.

17. Attach the outer petal with the veining facing towards you and the notch lined up over the base of the center, as for the inner petal. Smooth the outer petal where it attaches to the inner petal to secure. Continue to step 18.

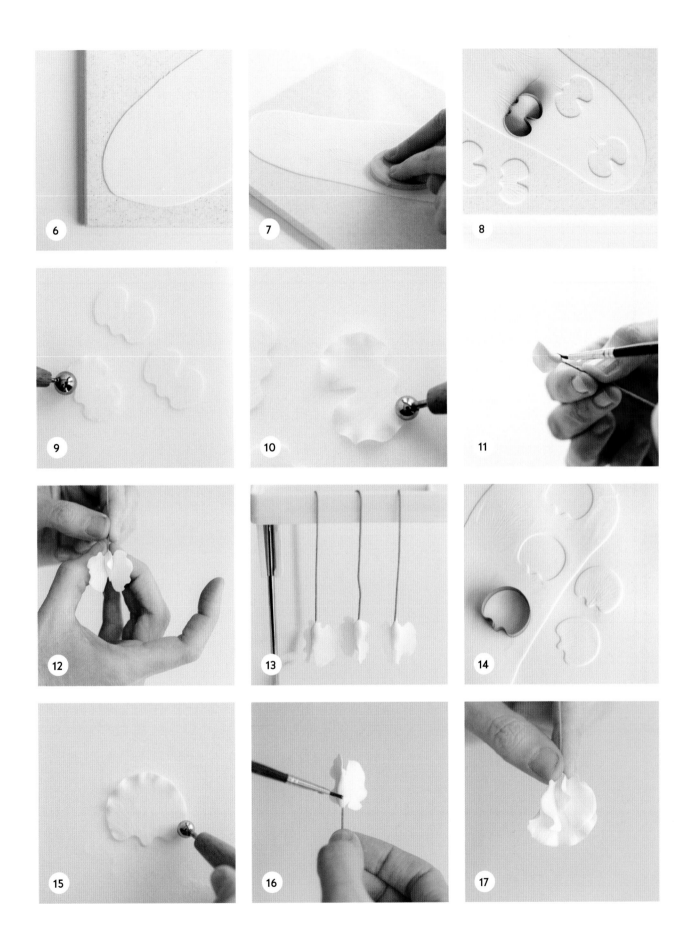

18. If desired, pinch the paste at the top center of the petal, creating a center vein.

19. Dry some of the sweet peas hanging so they are more closed.

20. Dry additional sweet peas lying face up on the backs of spoons so they are more open and fully bloomed.

MAKE THE CALYX

21. Roll green paste moderately thinly and keep it covered to prevent drying. Cut out several ⅝in (1.5cm) calyx shapes at a time.

22. Place the calyxes on a foam pad and widen each section with a small ball tool.

23. Pinch the tips of the calyx sections with your fingertips.

24. Apply a small amount of sugar glue on the calyx and slide up the wire to attach it to the base of the sweet pea. Press with your fingers to secure it around the base of the flower.

25. Glue a calyx to all of the sweet peas and buds, including all four stages of bloom. Allow them to dry completely before dusting.

DUST THE SWEET PEAS

26. Dust cosmos pink on the edges of all the petals, both front and back.

27. Dust a small amount of kiwi green on the reverse side of the petals, just above the calyx.

28. Dust kiwi green on the top and underside of the calyx.

29. Once all petals and calyxes are dusted, gently steam the sweet peas for a few seconds to set the color (see Getting Started). Let them dry before using.

tip

Sweet peas are also beautiful in white, and are quick to finish. Dust the backs of the petals and the calyxes with soft green, and then steam to set the color. Allow them to dry before using.

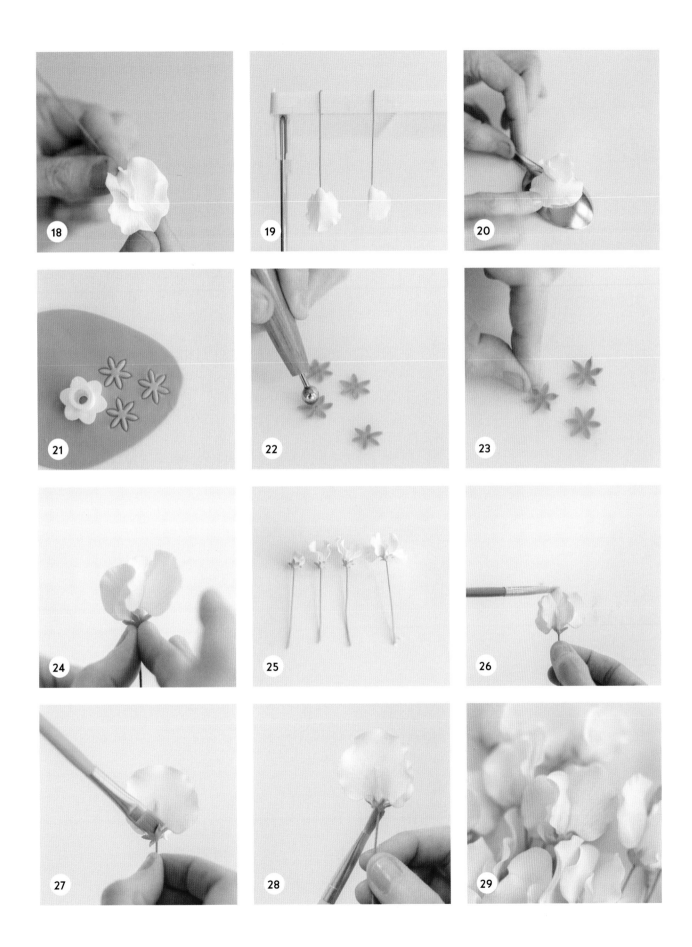

THE *Cake* PROJECTS

FOUNDATION LESSONS IN SUGAR FLOWER ARRANGING

These are the tips, tricks and techniques that have worked well for me in creating full and lush sugar flower arrangements. In the cake projects that follow we will be looking at specific types of arrangements, but these foundation lessons are a great place to start before you begin executing your first design.

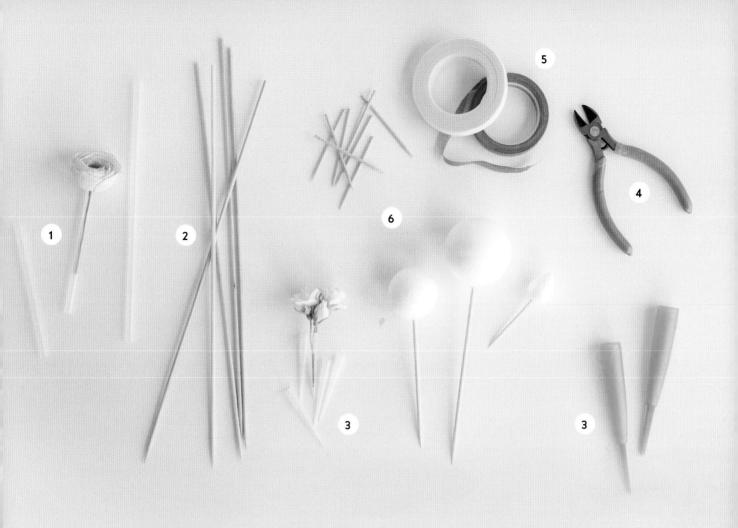

TOOLS & SUPPLIES

Make sure you have all of the tools and supplies you will need to create your arrangements. There are a number of different solutions for placing sugar flowers in cakes, and it's also good to know the guidelines provided by your local industry regulations and laws.

Supplies include: straws **(1)**, wooden skewers **(2)**, small and large flower piks **(3)**, wire cutters and pliers **(4)**, floral tape **(5)** and toothpicks **(6)**. You may also choose to add gloves to this list.

To use straws and flower piks, either position them in the cake first before adding flower stems, or insert your stems into them before placing in the cake. You may want to use a small amount of fondant or royal icing to secure the stems in the cavities. Small flowers can be taped to toothpicks, and larger flowers can be created on or taped to a wooden skewer. A longer skewer travels farther into a cake, providing counter-balance for a flower that is heavier or oversized.

COLOR & HARMONY

Lay out all of your finished flowers, filler flowers, buds and leaves, grouping them by color. Seeing everything together can help with visualizing the mood or overall effect the flowers will have when they are mixed together in your design. It's also great to see all of the pieces you have to work with so you can divide them accordingly. For smaller arrangements, you can also gather flowers and leaves together in your hands to see if you like certain colors or textures next to each other. I also suggest using photos of textiles and real flower arrangements as inspiration for both color palette and flower combinations, especially when you find some you really love!

FLOWER SHAPES

Take time to consider the shapes of your focal flowers. Some flowers are round, some have a base that comes to a point, and some flowers are more flat and open. The shapes of the flowers will affect how they can be arranged together. Some flowers fit together well, while others may need to be slightly manipulated to nestle together more closely (for example, make a slight bend in the

stems to make the flowers face away from each other). You may also be placing secondary and filler flowers next to a flower with an angled base, round shape, or underneath and around a more open, flat flower. As an example, cosmos flowers fit together well because of their v-shape, while ranunculus flowers are quite round but will fit together a bit better when slightly angled away from each other. The dahlia is usually a very flat and open flower, so if you want to use it with other flowers be sure to dry it in more of a v-shape.

SHAPES CREATED BETWEEN FLOWERS

You will also need to consider the shapes of the open spaces created when you put your focal flowers together, so you can decide what fillers might work best. There may be openings at the base of the flowers as well as at the top. Our essentials work perfectly to fill those gaps. The hydrangea flowers are created mostly in a v-shape so they can be nestled together closely in small groups to fill gaps between flowers. The little filler flowers have narrow tapered ends so they can fill tiny holes, and the all-purpose buds are little triangles that fit perfectly at the base of all of the flowers or even tucked under leaves.

FLOWER ARRANGING ORDER

1. Position and secure the focal flowers.

2. Place a small ball of fondant in the space between the focal flowers to insert the wires for the filler flowers and leaves. If desired, you can attach the fondant to the cake surface with a bit of water, sugar glue, royal icing or melted chocolate.

3. Fill the openings between the focal flowers with other small flowers, hydrangea flowers, all-purpose buds and leaves, sticking the wires into the ball of fondant. If a filler flower needs to face a certain direction to fill a gap, use tweezers to bend the wire.

4. Once the initial fillers and leaves are in place, begin filling the tiny holes with filler flowers and hydrangea buds. Continue to add filler flowers in layers to give the arrangement some depth and texture. Move on to the next opening and continue with the same process until all of the gaps are filled.

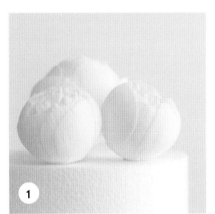

1

2

3

4

tips

If you are not sure about the techniques, take some time to practice on a dummy cake. Sometimes new solutions will show themselves during a practice run.

You will need more flowers than you think you do! Make sure you have enough to fill the gaps and always make extras to allow for breakage.

Another way to fill a gap is to use a freshly-made filler flower that is pliable enough to be wriggled into an opening without breaking. With larger flowers, you may just need to make the outer layer or two of petals fresh in order for the flowers to fit together well.

Remember, sometimes less is more. A beautifully crafted statement flower with a few leaves may be the perfect finishing touch.

SINGLE TIER ARRANGEMENTS
OFFSET ARRANGEMENT WITH
Closed Peonies & Lilacs

A beautiful single tier cake is perfect for many occasions from
birthdays and anniversaries, to intimate wedding celebrations.
A simple offset arrangement gives a design a focal point
that is natural and modern. This type of arrangement is
quick and easy with a single flower and a few bright leaves
placed delicately near the edge of a cake. If you want
to make it more elaborate, follow our simple techniques
for using multiple flowers and all of the pretty fillers.

TO CREATE THE CLOSED PEONIES & LILACS ARRANGEMENT YOU WILL NEED

CAKE TIER

- 7 x 6in (18 x 15cm) cake covered with white fondant
- 23in (60cm) of ¼in (5mm) white grosgrain ribbon
- Extra white fondant

FOCAL FLOWERS

- 3 closed peonies

FILLER FLOWERS, BUDS AND LEAVES

- 30 hydrangea flowers
- 10 all-purpose green buds
- 30 mixed lilacs (both open and cupped) plus a few extras
- 15 lilac buds
- 3 peony leaves
- 2 lilac leaves
- 5 greenery leaves

SPECIFIC SUPPLIES

- Floral tape (green)

1. Position and secure the closed peonies, offset on the top of the cake.

2. Gently press and secure a small amount of fondant between the peonies.

3. Position and insert the peony leaves and lilac leaves at the base of the peonies.

4. Fill the openings between the peonies with hydrangea and all-purpose buds.

5. Tape together almost all of the lilac flowers and lilac buds into a tight bouquet, leaving a few extras. Place the bouquet into the center opening between the three peonies, pushing the stem into the fondant between the flowers to secure. Use a few additional lilac flowers to fill any small holes.

6. Tape together the five greenery leaves at varying lengths. Position the leaves between two of the peonies, pushing the stem into the fondant between the flowers to secure. Let the leaves hang out a bit over the edge of the cake. Finish the cake with the ribbon (see Finishing Touches).

Make this variation of the offset arrangement using ranunculus and freesia and following the techniques for the closed peonies and lilacs cake.

tip

When working with round flowers like closed peonies or ranunculus, use all-purpose buds to fill in the small gaps around their bases. They are the perfect shape!

SINGLE TIER ARRANGEMENTS
OVER-THE-EDGE ARRANGEMENT WITH
Anemones

There is something extra lovely and romantic about sugar flowers spilling over the edge of a cake tier. If you haven't tried this type of arrangement, it can be as simple as taking three of the same flowers and positioning them on the top and side of a tier in a tight triangle shape, just like the garden roses version shown here. To give the arrangement a bit more detail like the anemone version, fill the spaces between the flowers with smaller blossoms, buds and leaves. To further build on the technique, use flowers of different sizes and varieties, and add trailing stems of blossoms or greenery cascading down the sides of the cake.

tip

If you are not sure about your arrangement, take a moment to place flowers on a styrofoam dummy to practice your design. Which flowers are at the top, and which flowers will cascade down the side?

TO CREATE THE ANEMONES ARRANGEMENT YOU WILL NEED

CAKE TIER

- 5 x 6in (13 x 15cm) cake covered with white fondant
- 17in (45cm) of ¼in (5mm) yellow-green grosgrain ribbon
- Extra white fondant

FOCAL FLOWERS

- 3 anemones

FILLER FLOWERS, BUDS AND LEAVES

- 2 large hydrangea leaves
- 2 small hydrangea leaves
- 9 all-purpose buds
- 9 filler flowers
- 10 hydrangea buds
- 15 hydrangea flowers

1. Position and secure the anemone flowers close to each other, with one at the edge of the tier, and the remaining two on the side. Looking from above, the three anemones will create a triangle shape.

2. Gently press and secure a small amount of fondant between the anemones.

3. Position and insert the hydrangea leaves at the base of the anemone flowers, letting some of them point down the tier from the flowers.

4. Begin filling the spaces between the anemones with all-purpose buds and hydrangea flowers. Fill any remaining tiny holes with the filler flowers. Finish the cake with the ribbon (see Finishing Touches).

Make this variation of the over-the-edge
arrangement using three garden roses and
two rose leaves, following the positioning
techniques for the anemones cake.

SINGLE TIER ARRANGEMENTS
FLORAL CROWN WITH
Cherry Blossom

Arrange delicate blossoms and buds in a crown around the top edge of a small cake for an adorable birthday or anniversary wish. The techniques here can be applied to a bigger cake using a mix of larger flowers and filler flowers, or use the small crown tier designs here as the top tier of a larger wedding cake.

tip

For the apple blossom design, use the same techniques substituting apple blossoms and buds, and arranging them on the same size cake tier covered with yellow-green fondant.

TO CREATE THE CHERRY BLOSSOM ARRANGEMENT YOU WILL NEED

CAKE TIER

- 4 x 6in (10 x 15cm) covered with white fondant
- Extra white fondant
- 14in (35cm) of ¼in (5mm) yellow-green grosgrain ribbon

BLOSSOMS, BUDS AND LEAVES

- 35 cherry blossoms
- 25 cherry blossom buds
- 2 cherry blossom leaves (plus extras if desired)

SPECIFIC SUPPLIES

- Sugar glue and brush
- Royal icing or melted white chocolate (optional)

1. Roll out a ball of the extra fondant into a long rope ½in (1cm) wide. Brush a circle of sugar glue ½in (1cm) in from the edge of the cake and gently attach the rope to the cake in a ring shape. Allow to set for a few minutes. Using wire cutters, begin trimming the wires for the cherry blossom flowers and buds and insert them into the fondant rope. To begin the crown, place a flower facing outwards, one facing inwards, and one on the top in between the two, and begin working your way around the cake top, filling in the circle and keeping the flowers as tight together as possible. If you are worried about the flowers staying in place, dip the wire ends in thick royal icing or cooled melted white chocolate, using it as "glue".

2. Once you have filled the rope with flowers, go back and fill in any open spaces with more buds and flowers as needed.

3. Add two leaves at the front of the cake by sliding their wires underneath the flowers and into the ring of fondant. Additional leaves may be added as desired. Finish the cake with the ribbon (see Finishing Touches).

Make this variation of the floral crown arrangement using sweet peas and hydrangea flowers, following the techniques for the cherry blossom cake.

MULTI TIER ARRANGEMENTS

WIDE LEDGE ARRANGEMENT WITH

Cosmos

Versatile and easy to decorate, the wide ledge is
the perfect place for a single large or oversized
flower, as well as large groups of flowers. The wider
ledge also makes it easy to build up lush bunches
of filler flowers around the focal flowers, so you
can create a full, stunning design effortlessly.

1

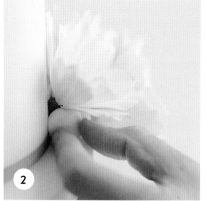

2

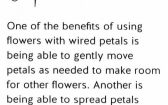

tip

One of the benefits of using flowers with wired petals is being able to gently move petals as needed to make room for other flowers. Another is being able to spread petals open to help hide small gaps.

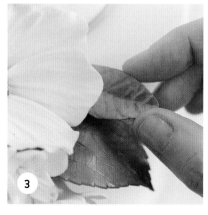

3

4

TO CREATE THE COSMOS ARRANGEMENT YOU WILL NEED

....

CAKE TIERS

- 4 x 5in (10 x 13cm) tier covered with white fondant
- 6 x 6in (15 x 15cm) tier covered with white fondant
- 35in (90cm) of ¼in (5mm) yellow-green grosgrain ribbon
- Extra white fondant

FOCAL FLOWERS

- 3 pink cosmos flowers
- 5 freesia flowers

FILLER FLOWERS, BUDS AND LEAVES

- 1 freesia stem with 3 green buds and 4 white buds
- 2 hydrangea leaves
- 2 sweet pea leaves
- 12 hydrangea flowers
- 3 all-purpose buds

1. Add the ribbon to both tiers before you arrange the flowers (see Finishing Touches). Position and secure the cosmos flowers on the ledge so they are nested together in a triangle shape. Position and secure the freesia flowers in the space between the two lower flowers. Position and secure the stem of freesia buds directly below the freesia flowers.

2. Gently press small balls of fondant on the ledge around the base of the cosmos flowers to insert the wires for the fillers.

3. Insert the hydrangea and sweet pea leaves at the base of the cosmos flowers.

4. Arrange the hydrangea flowers and buds to fill the gaps around the flowers, working on the ledges as well as a bit below the cosmos flowers.

Make this variation of the wide ledge arrangement using magnolia and hydrangea flowers and a variety of leaves, following the techniques for the cosmos cake.

MULTI TIER ARRANGEMENTS
NARROW LEDGE ARRANGEMENT WITH

Ranunculus

Narrow ledges are fresh and modern, and the most popular cake style at Petalsweet. Generally, the narrow ledges lend themselves to smaller flowers, delicate arrangements and flowers that are shaped flat or open, but they are also perfect for a single cupped round flower surrounded by a handful of fillers and a few leaves tucked in at the base. The options are endless and always stylish. If you do use larger flowers, be sure they are anchored well into the cake to prevent any shifting or tearing.

TO CREATE THE RANUNCULUS ARRANGEMENT YOU WILL NEED

CAKE TIERS

- 4 x 5in (10 x 13cm) tier covered with white fondant
- 5 x 6in (13 x 15cm) tier covered with white fondant
- 31in (80cm) of ¼in (5mm) yellow-green grosgrain ribbon
- Extra white fondant

FOCAL FLOWERS

- 1 large ranunculus flower (with 6 layers of petals plus extra open petals to make a 2in/5cm flower)
- 1 smaller ranunculus flower (with 4 layers of petals plus open petals to make a 1½in/4cm flower)

FILLER FLOWERS, BUDS AND LEAVES

- 6 hydrangea flowers
- 7 filler flowers
- 1 filler flower bud
- 3 all-purpose buds
- 3 hydrangea leaves
- 2 sweet pea leaves

1. Prepare the cake tiers, then add the ribbon (see Finishing Touches).

2. Position the two ranunculus flowers next to each other slightly offset to one side. The larger flower is the main focus, and the smaller flower is tucked slightly behind it.

3. Gently press some small balls of extra fondant on the ledge around the base of the flowers to insert the fillers and leaves. Fill in the spaces around and in between the ranunculus flowers with the hydrangea and buds. Tuck the two sweet pea leaves into the right side of the smaller flower.

4. Finish by layering the filler flowers over the hydrangea and buds, filling in any small gaps.

MULTI TIER ARRANGEMENTS
THREE TIERS WITH
Charm Peonies

A simple way to create a clean, well balanced three tier design is by using a smaller arrangement on or near the top of the cake, and a larger arrangement between the lower two tiers, as shown on both cakes here. You can easily apply the same concept to a cake design with more tiers, creating larger arrangements as you work from the top down to the base. To broaden the design elements, browse the techniques from the single tier and multi tier cake projects to find the arrangement styles you love, and put them together to create your own work of art.

TO CREATE THE CHARM PEONIES ARRANGEMENT YOU WILL NEED

CAKE TIERS

- 5 x 5in (13 x 13cm) tier covered with white fondant
- 7 x 5in (18 x 13cm) tier covered with white fondant
- 8 x 6in (20 x 15cm), covered with white fondant
- 67in (170cm) of ¼in (5mm) yellow-green grosgrain ribbon
- Extra white fondant

FOCAL FLOWERS

- 3 charm peonies, 1 large, 1 medium and 1 small
- 2 cosmos flowers
- 2 peony buds

FILLER FLOWERS, BUDS AND LEAVES

- 8 freesia flowers divided into groups of 5 and 3
- 2 freesia bud stems buds
- 56 hydrangea flowers
- 16 all-purpose buds
- 10 hydrangea buds
- 45 filler flowers
- 1 stem of 3 filler flower buds taped with 2 filler flower leaves
- 1 small stem of 3 sweet pea flowers taped with 2 sweet pea buds
- 8 hydrangea leaves

1. Prepare the cake tiers and add the ribbon (see Finishing Touches). Position and secure the large and small charm peonies offset on the lower tier ledge, and then position the medium charm peony offset in the opposite direction on the top tier.

2. Position and secure the secondary flowers, including adding a cosmos and a peony bud to the top arrangement. Position and secure the second cosmos on the lower ledge next to the large peony, and the peony bud between and just below the two peony flowers.

3. Position and secure the freesia flowers, placing a group of five flowers between the two peonies on the lower tier, and a group of three flowers between the peony and cosmos on the top tier. After securing the flowers, add a freesia bud stem just underneath both groupings of freesia.

4. Gently press small balls of fondant around the base and in between the peony flowers, cosmos and freesia to insert the wires for the fillers. Start by inserting a few of the hydrangea leaves in place under and out to the sides of the peonies. Fill the spaces between the flowers with the hydrangea, hydrangea buds and all-purpose buds. Fill any remaining small holes with the filler flowers, layering them on top of each other to add texture and depth.

5. Finish by inserting any remaining leaves at the base and outer edges of the arrangements. Insert the filler flower bud stem and sweet pea stem in the top of the arrangement to add visual interest.

tip

Positioning the lower flowers first will make it a bit easier to find the best placement for the top tier flower. If you are not sure about placement of the peonies, hold a lightly crumpled ball of clean paper above and around the tiers, moving it around until you find good spots for the flowers. Mark the fondant lightly with a toothpick or modeling tool and secure the flowers in place. If you drop the paper ball, there is no damage to the cake, and no risk of broken flowers!

tip

Use the filler flowers in small groups of five to seven, taped together to fill gaps between the larger flowers more quickly, or use them as single blossoms to fill tiny openings between the hydrangea petals.

PRE-MADE ARRANGEMENTS
DOMED TOPPER WITH
Peonies & Ranunculus

If you want to make a floral arrangement ahead of time, try using styrofoam for a pre-made cake topper. Working on styrofoam allows you to arrange your flowers, change your mind, and re-arrange them again! The dome topper here is 5 inches (13cm) wide, and made to sit atop a 4-inch (10cm) cake that is the top tier in a larger design, but it can easily be scaled up in size as needed. The topper will have some weight, so be sure to provide adequate internal structure in the cake to support the topper.

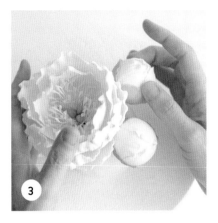

tip

I find it helpful to have a model of the exact cake sizes in styrofoam dummies to make sure the piece I am creating will remain in proportion to the overall design and tier sizes.

TO CREATE THE PEONIES & RANUNCULUS DOMED TOPPER YOU WILL NEED

CAKE TIER

- 4 x 4in (10 x 10cm) tier covered with white fondant
- 3in (7.5cm) aerated styrofoam ball
- 7in (18cm) styrofoam dummy
- Wooden skewers
- Hot glue gun or royal icing
- Sugar flowers, buds and leaves
- Adequate dowel support in cake
- Extra fondant to match the cake

BLOSSOMS, BUDS AND LEAVES

- 1 ruffled peony
- 3 peony buds
- 3 ranunculus flowers
- 65 hydrangea flowers
- 20 all-purpose buds
- 10 hydrangea buds
- 60 filler flowers
- 4 large hydrangea leaves
- 4 small hydrangea leaves
- 5 greenery leaves taped together in a bunch

1. To fit on a 4in (10cm) cake tier, cut a 3in (7.5cm) aerated styrofoam ball in half and cover with fondant to match the cake. Secure two skewers into the flat base of the styrofoam with the hot glue gun or royal icing.

2. To arrange the flowers, gently push the skewers into a styrofoam dummy to hold the dome firmly in place. Begin by positioning the open peony slightly offset from the center of the dome. Pre-poke holes as needed with a skewer.

3. Add the three peony buds and three ranunculus flowers spaced around the dome as desired.

4. Fill in the spaces between the flowers with hydrangea flowers and buds, all-purpose buds and filler flowers, working down to the bottom edge of the dome. Leave a small space empty to lift up the topper from the dummy with a spatula. Slide your fingers underneath the topper to move it, and secure it on the doweled cake with the two skewers.

5. Finish the topper by completely filling in any remaining spaces and the bottom edge with flowers and leaves so they hide the styrofoam ball and spill over the top edge of the cake tier as desired.

PRE-MADE ARRANGEMENTS
FLORAL SEPARATOR WITH
Climbing Roses

A beautiful way to add height and texture to your design, the floral separator isn't only reserved for the grandest of wedding cakes. This pretty little project is a great way to practice the construction process and work on arranging smaller flowers with fillers, buds and leaves. The band of flowers is gorgeous on its own, or you can create an additional arrangement as shown here.

TO CREATE THE CLIMBING ROSES FLORAL SEPARATOR YOU WILL NEED

CAKE TIERS

- 5 x 5in (13 x 13cm) tier covered with white fondant, with ⅜in (8mm) hole in the center of the bottom cake board
- 6 x 4in (15 x 10cm) tier covered with white fondant, doweled, and with ⅜in (8mm) hole in the center of the bottom cake board
- 7 x 5in (18 x 13cm) tier covered with white fondant, doweled, and with ⅜in (8mm) hole in the center of the bottom cake board

FLOWERS FOR SEPARATOR

- 20 climbing roses (mix of sizes)
- 15 climbing rose buds
- 35 cherry blossoms
- 25 cherry blossom buds
- 50 hydrangea flowers
- 15 hydrangea buds
- 60 filler flowers
- 12 all-purpose buds
- 5 small rose leaves

FLOWERS FOR TOP ARRANGEMENT

- 4 climbing roses
- 3 cherry blossoms
- 3 cherry blossom buds
- 7 hydrangea flowers
- 5 filler flowers
- 2 all-purpose buds
- 2 small rose leaves

SPECIFIC SUPPLIES

- Extra white fondant
- 9 x ¼in (23cm x 5mm) diameter masonite cake board, with ⅜in (8mm) hole drilled in center, covered with white fondant
- Craft knife
- Hot glue gun
- ⅜in (8mm) dowel cut to 15in (38cm) long, sharpened to a point on one end
- Two 7in (18cm) cardboard cake boards with ⅜in (8mm) hole in center
- Two 4in (10cm) cardboard cake boards with ¾–1in (2–2.5cm) hole in center (the holes are larger so the finished separator can be adjusted to the right or left between the cake tiers as needed)
- 4 x 2in (10 x 5cm) styrofoam disc with ¾in (2cm) hole in center
- 90in (225cm) of ¼in (5mm) yellow-green grosgrain ribbon
- Sugar glue or water
- Toothpicks (cocktail sticks) or needle tool
- Extra 7 x 6in (18 x 15cm) styrofoam dummy to use as a platform for the separator while you are filling it with flowers

1. To make the separator, use a small amount of glue to attach the 4in (10cm) cardboard cake boards to the 4in (10cm) styrofoam disc, making sure the center holes line up. Allow to dry.

2. Roll a strip of fondant 3in (7.5cm) wide x 14in (35.5cm) long x ⅛in (3mm) thick. Apply a small amount of sugar glue or water to the fondant and wrap it around the separator, covering both the styrofoam and the edges of the cardboard. Trim off excess with a craft knife.

3. Center the fondant-covered separator between the two 7in (18cm) cardboard cake boards and place on top of the extra 7in (18cm) dummy. Push the ⅜in (8mm) dowel down through the center holes just far enough to secure it to the dummy. The two cardboards will act as a guide for positioning the flowers so they don't break when the cake tiers are stacked.

4. Gather your sugar flowers, buds and leaves, and begin arranging them in the separator by sticking the wires into the styrofoam. Use a toothpick or needle tool to pre-poke holes if needed.

5. Continue adding roses, cherry blossoms, hydrangea and buds as you work around the separator, and then layering over the small gaps between them with filler flowers.

6. Continue working between the cardboard guides to fill the separator completely with roses, cherry blossoms, hydrangea and buds.

7. Secure the center dowel into the cake board with glue. Stack and secure the bottom 7 x 5in (18 x 13cm) tier over the center dowel. Gently remove the cardboard guides from the floral separator and carefully add it on top of the bottom tier. Stack and secure the remaining two cake tiers on top of the separator, sliding

them down over the center dowel. Add a few more flowers, buds and leaves around the lower edge of the separator to fill any gaps, letting some of the flowers and leaves spill down over the top edge of the bottom cake tier.

8. Measure and attach the ribbon to the base of each cake tier and the cake board (see Finishing Touches).

9. With the ribbon in place, now go back to fill in any gaps along the top edge of the separator with additional small flowers and buds.

10. Create a small offset arrangment on the top cake tier by securing a few of the roses in the cake and surrounding them with a few small balls of fondant. Insert the wires for the remaining flowers, buds and leaves into the fondant to create a nice arrangement.

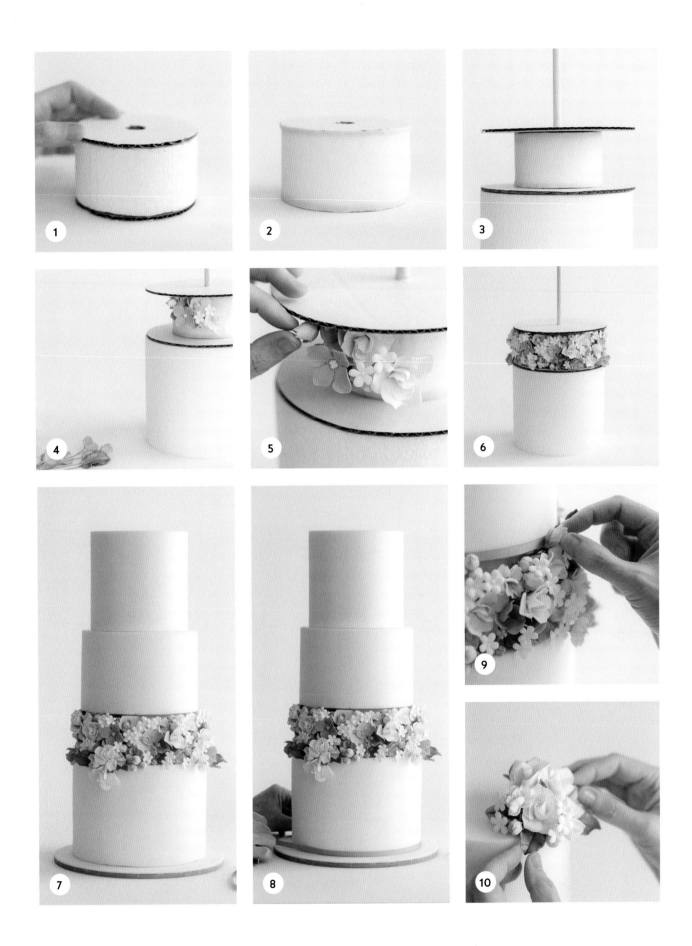

Finishing touches

We use real ribbon to finish most of our cake tiers and really love narrower widths in simple colors that complement our color palette. A lovely yellow-green color is one of the most versatile with all of our flowers, but we also like pale pinks, soft neutral tones, chocolate grosgrain with white stitching, and an occasional black or striped ribbon for a tailored finish. Don't worry about having every color; a few good basics will be very versatile.

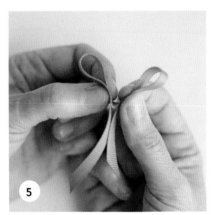

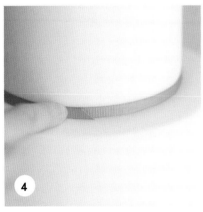

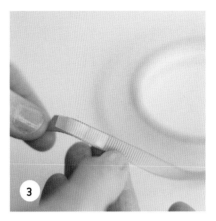

SPECIFICS YOU WILL NEED

···

- Ribbon
- Scissors
- Double-sided tape in same or narrower width as ribbon
- Finished cake tiers (or same size dummies)
- String
- Ruler or measuring tape (optional)

1. To measure the length of ribbon needed, gently wrap the ribbon around the base of the finished cake tier (or same size dummy tier), allowing an extra 1in (2.5cm) overlap. Alternatively use a piece of string to make this measurement.

2. Trim the ribbon to size cutting the end at an angle using sharp scissors.

3. Cut a ¾in (2cm) piece of the double-sided tape and attach one side to the ribbon.

4. Wrap the ribbon around the cake with the ends overlapping at the back. Peel off the second covering on the tape, and secure in place on top of the other end so the tape is only touching the ribbon.

5. If you want to hide the place where the ribbon joins, tie a small bow with a piece of ribbon that has been neatly trimmed at both ends.

6. Attach a small loop of tape on the back of the bow and secure in place. If desired, the bow can be used as a delicate addition to the cake design by being placed in the front.

SUPPLIERS

USA

CAKES BY DESIGN/SCOTT WOOLLEY
www.worldofsugarart.com
Cutters, single-sided veiners, stamens,
sugarcraft tools and supplies

CK PRODUCTS
www.ckproducts.com
Essential and specialty supplies, Celbuds,
petal dust, plastic half sphere formers

CRYSTAL COLORS
www.sugarpaste.com
Petal dust (Kiwi, Moss Green, Holly, Peach,
Cream)

FIRST IMPRESSIONS MOLDS
www.firstimpressionsmolds.com
Silicone leaf and petal veiners

GLOBAL SUGAR ART
www.globalsugarart.com
Extensive range of tools and supplies,
masonite cake boards, cutters, veiners,
confectioner's glaze, gel colors, petal dust

**INTERNATIONAL SUGAR ART
COLLECTION**
www.nicholaslodge.com
Flower and leaf cutters, veiners, sugarcraft
tools and supplies, tylose, leaf glaze

MICHAEL'S CRAFT STORES
www.michaels.com
Aerated styrofoam balls, dusting brushes.
Celebrate It brand ribbon (yellow-green,
chocolate grosgrain and white)

PASTRY CHEF CENTRAL
www.pastrychef.com
Plastic half sphere molds

SMOOTHFOAM
www.smoothfoam.com
High-density styrofoam balls

SUGAR DELITES
www.sugardelites.com
Cutters, veiners, confectioner's glaze, floral
wire/tape, sugarcraft tools, gel colors

SUNFLOWER SUGAR ART
www.sunflowersugarartusa.com
Cutters, veiners, silicone molds

SUGAR ART STUDIO
www.sugarartstudio.com
Cutters, veiners, silicone molds

UK/EUROPE

SQUIRES KITCHEN SHOP
www.squires-shop.com
Cutters, Orchard Products cutters, Great
Impressions veiners, gel colors, petal dust,
leaf glaze, essential tools, stamens, flower piks

A PIECE OF CAKE
www.sugaricing.com
Essential and specialty tools and supplies

MARCEL VELDBLOEM FLOWER VEINERS
www.flowerveiners.nl
Rose petal veiners, flower and leaf veiners

CANADA

FLOUR CONFECTIONS
www.flourconfections.com
Extensive range of tools and supplies, half
sphere/petal formers, drying foam, stamens,
cutters, petal dust

THANK YOU

Thank you so much to the talented
team at F&W Media for the production
of this book. To Ame Verso for the
amazing opportunity, Anna Wade for
her creative direction and making the
layouts beautiful, Jane Trollope for
patiently editing all of my written text,
and Jeni Hennah for helping me pull it
all together to get to the finish line.

I'm so grateful to Nathan Rega and Kira
Friedman at Harper Point Photography
for understanding Petalsweet and
taking so many beautiful photos to help
me to convey my artistry and message.

Thank you so much to these amazing
artists, many of whom have been my
teachers and mentors, and are my
colleagues and friends, and are some
of the most inspiring people I know:
Colette Peters, Scott Woolley, Nicholas
Lodge, Ron Ben Israel, Greg Cleary,
Giovanna Smith, Robert Haynes,
Naomi Yamamoto and Alan Dunn.

I am so grateful to all of my students
for the wonderful experiences in
classes and workshops; watching you
enjoy the process of making pretty
sugar flowers is my happiness.

Much love and thank you to my mom
and step-dad, family and friends
for supporting my dreams and
encouraging my artfulness. And to my
dad, who isn't here to see this book,
but listened to my early visions and
asked me about it all the time.

And finally, my love and gratitude to
my incredible husband Keith, the best
Senior Executive Intern I could ever ask
for. Your support, encouragement and
love are everything to me.

ABOUT THE AUTHOR

Owner, artist and Creative Director at Petalsweet, based in San Diego,
California, Jacqueline is a wedding cake artist turned sugarcraft and cake
decorating Instructor. After falling in love with sugar flowers as a hobby,
Jacqueline studied with some of the best sugar flower makers in the
business, and soon after began her journey in cake. Officially founded in
2005, Petalsweet cakes are known for their clean and modern designs,
decorated with delicate, stylized sugar flowers in soft pastel color palettes.
Thrilled to share her love for the art form, Jacqueline dedicates most
of her time to teaching her signature style of cake decorating and sugar
flowers, traveling throughout the States and internationally.

www.petalsweet.com

INDEX

A SEWANDSO BOOK
© F&W Media International, Ltd 2017

SewandSo is an imprint of F&W Media International, Ltd
Pynes Hill Court, Pynes Hill, Exeter, EX2 5AZ

F&W Media International, Ltd is a subsidiary of F+W Media, Inc
10151 Carver Road, Suite #200, Blue Ash, OH 45242, USA

Text and Designs © Jacqueline Butler 2017
Layout and Photography © F&W Media International, Ltd 2017

First published in the UK and USA in 2017

A catalogue record for this book is available from the British Library.

ISBN-13: 978-1-4463-0646-8 hardback
SRN: R4952 hardback

ISBN-13: 978-1-4463-7503-7 PDF
SRN: R5022 PDF

ISBN-13: 978-1-4463-7502-0 EPUB
SRN: R5023 EPUB

Printed in China by RR Donnelley for:
F&W Media International, Ltd
Pynes Hill Court, Pynes Hill, Exeter, EX2 5AZ

10 9 8 7 6 5 4 3 2 1

Content Director: Ame Verso
Senior Editor: Jeni Hennah
Project Editor: Jane Trollope
Proofreader: Cheryl Brown
Design and Art Direction: Anna Wade
Junior Designer: Ali Stark
Photography: Nathan Rega
Production Manager: Beverley Richardson

F&W Media publishes high quality books on a wide range of subjects.
For more great book ideas visit: www.sewandso.co.uk

Layout of the digital edition of this book may vary depending on reader hardware and display settings.